GRILLING AND BARBEQUE GUIDE

For Hoagie - Keep the Fires Burnin'

Portions of this book were originally published in <u>Absolute Barbeque</u>, and are reprinted here with the written consent of Old Market Press.

This special edition has been created for the limited use of The Kansas City Steak Company by Old Market Press.

KANSAS CITY STEAK COMPANY - GRILLING AND BARBEQUE GUIDE
>Original Recipes by: Bill Venable and Rick Welch
>Edited by: Bill Venable, Rick Welch and Bruce Daniel
>Cover Design by: Eddie Scavuzzo

First Printing

KANSAS CITY STEAK COMPANY - GRILLING AND BARBEQUE GUIDE
ISBN 1-882907-06-X

9   8   7   6   5   4   3   2   1   0

Printed in the United States of America

Old Market Press
a River City Products, Inc. Company
113 West 14th Avenue
North Kansas City, MO 64116
(816)472-4363

Kansas City Steak Company
2501 Guinotte Avenue
PO Box 33442
Kansas City, MO 64120
(800)524-1844 In Kansas City call
(816)842-BEEF AKA (816)842-2333

Table of Contents

Kansas City Steak Company

Congratulations on your good taste and wise investment! The Kansas City Steak Company provides not only the finest in meat, but with this Special Edition book, you'll be able to prepare and serve the best steaks on earth!

Thawing Instructions:

Please DON'T:

DO NOT use a microwave or soak your steaks in water to hasten thawing. Doing so will impair the rich flavor and affect the tenderness that makes Kansas City Steak Company cuts so special.

Please DO:

DO thaw your steaks ONLY in the refrigerator for 18 to 24 hours. We know its hard to wait, but refrigerator thawing actually enhances the flavor by preserving the natural tenderness of the meat. The slow thawing process brings the steaks back to their natural reddish-brown color. As you will notice, the color will be darker than the red meat you are accustomed to seeing in the supermarket. This color change is the natural result of the careful aging process -- experts look for the rich, reddish brown color to identify a truly fine cut of meat.

Incidentally, it is possible that there was no dry ice remaining in the insulated cooler when your steaks arrived. If so, do not be concerned. As long as the steaks still feel cool to the touch, you may either refreeze or refrigerate them. They can be cooked later with confidence.

Kansas City Steaks: The World's Best

Nothing challenges the supremacy of steak when it comes to grilled foods. The simple elegance of richly-colored, aromatic Kansas City Strips, Ribeyes, T-Bones, Porterhouse or Filet Mignon provides the ideal in appearance and flavor, tenderness and taste. The properly prepared steak is the epitome of the grilling art.

The following tips will make it possible for you to attain flavorful, easily repeatable results when preparing steaks from the Kansas City Steak Company.

Before Grilling: Recommendations

If desired, marinate steaks using any of your favorite recipes or those included in this book. Times range from 15 to 20 minutes with the sample spices included with your steak order, to as long as 6 to 8 hours with some recipe ideas. Marinades penetrate meat fibers, enabling the meat to become tenderized and flavored.

Note: Marinades and sauces may be used as a baste during the grilling process, but those high in sugar or other ingredients that burn easily should be brushed on only during the last few minutes of cooking time.

Regardless of whether or not a marinade is used, DO NOT cut indentations into steaks or poke them with a fork in an attempt to tenderize them. The results will be the opposite of what is desired -- natural juices, which enhance flavor and allow the meat to retain its moisture, will be lost and the meat will become more dry and less tender.

Essentials For Your Success

A key to grilling success is control of temperature. For this simple reason, allow steaks to reach room temperature before grilling.

The major key to grilling success is using direct and indirect heat correctly. Ideally, steaks are first seared over direct heat, then placed over indirect heat for the remainder of the cooking time.

Whether using a gas grill or conventional unit with a charcoal or wood fire, the technique is the same. Build the fire on one side of the grill only. On units where the grill can be positioned up and down, the ideal fire to grill surface distance is three inches.

For charcoal fires, allow the briquette to burn down until they are completely gray -- this assures you the fire is producing maximum heat, which is also key to grilling success.

Grilling Kansas City Steaks

Once your fire is ready, place the steak directly over the flames and sear each side for 45 to 60 seconds.

Move the steak away from the fire to the middle of the opposite grill side. Close or cover the grill, leaving air vents open.

The following tables are close approximations for grilling times for our premium Kansas City aged beef products. The times listed do not include searing time.

As an example: After searing, a rare 8 ounce 3/4 inch thick Kansas City Strip steak would be cooked six minutes, then flipped and cooked six more minutes; thus, the 6-6 designation below.

The following tables will serve as your guide to successful grilling times:

Kansas City Strip, Ribeye, Porterhouse, & T-Bone	Thickness	Rare	Medium Rare	Medium
	3/4 inch	6-6	8-6	8-8
	1 inch	7-7	9-7	9-9
	1 1/4 inch	8-8	10-8	10-10
	1 1/2 inch	9-9	12-9	12-12

Filet Mignon	Thickness	Rare	Medium Rare	Medium
	1 1/4 inch	4-4	5-4	5-5
	1 1/2 inch	5-5	6-5	6-6
	1 3/4 inch	6-6	7-6	7-7

While weather and other conditions may affect the times slightly, the above are good reference points.

After grilling, remove steaks from grill and allow to rest for five to ten minutes before slicing across the grain.

Kansas City Steaks - The Best There Are

Kansas City was a livestock center for over 120 years, when Texas ranchers first drove their cattle north to feed on the blue stem grass of our prairies. Missouri and Kansas with their lush prairie grasses and rich growing region for feed corn, produced the highest quality beef cattle. Kansas City, located right in the middle of the region, became one of the largest livestock centers in the world, and gained a reputation for the finest steaks available. It was to this center that my great grandfather came in 1932 to set up a business distributing the "best steaks there are."

Our family is now in its sixth generation of service in the beef industry. Generation after generation, we have been offering the finest quality aged beef and our assurance of reliable service. This has become a family tradition.

"These steaks are the best there are" is an extravagant statement, but it is based on sound reason. My great grandfather's business was to supply steaks to the finest restaurants right in the heart of steak country. The people around here know good steak and insist on only the finest beef. In turn, the best restaurants from around the country have come to us to satisfy their patrons. It is the same Kansas City restaurant quality steak my great grandfather sold that we offer today.

We have accumulated quite an impressive list of customers over the years including famous politicians, entertainers, sports figures and the list goes on and on. They know its no accident that the finest beef comes from Kansas City, and they depend on us to supply the beef they desire.

We use only midwestern corn fed premium beef for our catalog shipments. To be considered good enough for the Kansas City Steak Company label of excellence, the beef must pass rigid grading and quality standards for marbling and texture.

We then age the beef for the optimum number of days at controlled temperatures. The aging gives our Kansas City steaks their unusual tenderness and flavor. And it is this aging that you cannot find in any supermarket or butcher shop.

Time is our only additive. No chemicals are ever used to tenderize our steaks or give them flavor. Our steaks are flash-frozen to lock in the juice and freshness; no preservatives are ever added.

Every steak is hand-cut and trimmed by our expert craftsmen, some of whom have practiced their craft for as long as forty years. Their knowledge is an assurance of value to you, our customers.

Value to our customers is our family goal. It is this value that we make available to you by shipping our famous Kansas City beef around the country and the world. This value can be recognized in all aspects of our service, from the excellence of our beef to the Federal Express delivery to your door.

Enjoy Your Order and This Gift to You!

The result of our efforts is a tender, juicy steak with the rich flavor that only natural aging can provide. We invite you to enjoy Kansas City steaks and share them with your family, friends and customers. To assure you that our products are truly "the best there are," we offer you our unconditional money back guarantee.

This book has been put together by our friends, the members of the Kansas City Barbeque Inner Circle. They are driven to the delivery of absolute barbeque perfection just as we are driven to the delivery of perfect Kansas City aged beef. Please enjoy these mouth watering recipes and try them on the next shipment you receive from the Kansas City Steak Company.

Cordially,

Edward Scavuzzo

Kansas City Steaks With Red Wine Sauce

1 shallot
1 cup beef stock
1/8 teaspoon thyme
1 1/2 cup red wine
2 tablespoons butter or margarine
2 tablespoons flour
salt and pepper
6 Kansas City Strip Steaks

In a sauce pan boil and reduce half of the red wine. Add stock. Sauté minced shallot in butter. When shallot is almost translucent, add a pinch of thyme and flour. Cook on low heat for about 10 minutes, stirring often. Add the remaining red wine to the stock mixture stirring constantly. Cook slowly for about 10 to 15 minutes. Add salt and pepper to taste.

Grill steaks over hot grill, searing 1 minute on each side and cooking over indirect heat for 6 minutes on one side, flip and cook 8 minutes on the other for medium rare. Drizzle a little sauce over steaks during the final minutes of cooking. Serve with remaining wine sauce.

Lori & Steve's Chateaubriand

4 pounds beef tenderloin
1 clove garlic, crushed
1/4 cup sea salt
1/4 cup cracked black pepper
1 bay leaf
2 onions, sliced
1/2 cup olive oil

Rub the Chateaubriand with sea salt and cracked black pepper. Place meat in a glass dish with bay leaf, onion and garlic. Cover with oil. Marinate in refrigerator for 2 to 3 hours, turning every 45 minutes. Drain and sear over a hot fire for about 2 minutes on each side.

Finish over slow heat for about 25 minutes.

Joan's Primo Prime Rib Roast

4 to 5 pound beef prime rib roast
2 teaspoons grated orange peel
2 cloves garlic, crushed
2 tablespoons sea salt
1 teaspoon cracked black pepper
1 teaspoon dried thyme leaves, crushed

Combine orange peel, garlic, sea salt and pepper. Rub mixture evenly over surface of roast. Place roast in a foil pan, fat side up, on a wire rack. Insert a meat thermometer into the thickest part of the roast.

Place pan on indirect side of grill, leaving alternate side on high. Wood chips may be added to the hot side of the grill for extra smoke flavor.

Cook on a hot grill (300 to 350 degrees) for about 18 to 20 minutes per pound. Thermometer will register 135 degrees for rare and 155 degrees for medium. Remove roast at appropriate temperature. Cover with a foil tent and let stand for 15 to 20 minutes. Temperature will continue to rise to reach 140 degrees for rare and 150 degrees for medium. Trim excess fat before carving.

Tai's Sweet And Sour Kansas City T-Bones

1/2 teaspoon sesame oil
1/2 teaspoon canola oil
1/2 onion, minced
1 jalapeno pepper, chopped fine
1 ounce fresh ginger root
zest of 1 large orange
1/2 teaspoon thyme
1/2 teaspoon oregano
12 ounces orange juice concentrate
4 T-bone steaks

Preheat oils in sauce pan then add onion, jalapeno pepper, ginger, orange zest, thyme and oregano. Sauté for about five minutes on low heat. Add orange juice and cook for another 15 minutes on a slow fire.

Grill steaks over hot grill, searing 1 minute on each side and cooking over indirect heat for 6 minutes on one side, flip and cook 8 minutes on the other for medium rare. Drizzle a little sauce over steaks during final minutes of cooking. Serve with remaining sweet and sour sauce.

Trés Speciale Kansas City Filet Mignon

4 bacon wrapped filet mignons
1/2 cup extra virgin olive oil
1 onion, chopped
1 teaspoon thyme
1/2 teaspoon salt
1 teaspoon garlic powder
1/4 teaspoon coarse ground black pepper
1/4 teaspoon ground red pepper

Coat filets with olive oil and place in a clean glass dish, set aside. Mix dry spices in a small bowl or mortar and pestle, then add onion. Rub spice mixture into each side of steaks, return to dish and refrigerate for one hour.

Sear over hot grill for about 1 minute on each side. Cook over indirect heat for 6 minutes on one side, flip and cook 8 minutes on the other for medium rare. Drizzle with remaining marinade mixture during last minutes of cooking.

Rick, Bill & Bruce's Kansas City Grilled Ribeye

6 Ribeye Steaks
1 stick butter or margarine
1 cup extra virgin olive oil
1 cup Merlot
1 large onion, minced
1/2 teaspoon rosemary
1 teaspoon basil
1/4 teaspoon salt
1/2 teaspoon ground black pepper
1/2 teaspoon ground red pepper
1 pound sliced fresh mushrooms

Sear steaks over hot gas grill for about 1 minute on each side. Cook over indirect heat for 6 minutes on one side, flip and cook 8 minutes on the other for medium rare.

Place a large iron skillet on your gas grill. When steaks are about half way done, heat butter and oil in the pan until smooth. Stir in onion and heat until tender. Add mushrooms and continue to cook until they change in color. Make sure to stay at the grill while cooking mushrooms as they can overcook easily. Add wine and spices as color turns. Remove from heat and serve at once.

The iron skillet on the grill is a great presentation touch while entertaining on the patio or deck.

Mimi's Grilled Tenderloin Tips Supreme

1/2 cup fat free Italian dressing
1 cup white vinegar
2 pounds tenderloin tips
1 onion, minced
1 teaspoon garlic powder
1 teaspoon salt
1 teaspoon ground black pepper
1 teaspoon ground red pepper
1 teaspoon paprika

Rub tenderloin tips with half of white vinegar and half of Italian dressing. Combine spices with remaining vinegar and dressing. Pour over tips. Continue to rub spices into the tips and let set for about half an hour in the refrigerator.

Place two to three hand-fulls of damp hickory chips on the lava rocks on the hot side of the grill and a large foil or tin pan of water on top of the lava rocks, directly over the fire. Sear tips over the hot side of the grill, about two to three minutes on each side, then move to the cold side of the grill and close the lid.

The cooking process should take about an hour on high heat. Keep the tips close to each other to help retain moisture. Every fifteen minutes sprinkle the remaining baste mixture on the tips. Cook until internal temperature reaches 135 degrees.

Grilled Lemon & Orange Porterhouse

4 - 1 inch thick Porterhouse steaks
1 cup red wine
1 clove garlic
2 lemons, sliced
2 oranges, sliced
1 onion, sliced
1 teaspoon ground black pepper
1/4 teaspoon salt

Lay fruit and onion slices in a small flat dish. Cover with wine, garlic, salt and pepper and allow to marinade for about one hour. After one hour add steak to mixture and place in refrigerator. Marinate in refrigerator for about one hour, turning steaks occasionally.

Grill over a hot fire, searing on each side for about one minute. Cook on indirect side of grill 8 to 10 minutes on each side, or until internal temperature reaches 135 degrees for perfect medium rare.

Bobby's Grilled Stuffed Prime Rib

1/2 cup fat free Italian dressing
1/4 cup fat free butter or margarine
1/4 cup minced onions
1/4 teaspoon salt substitute
1 cup sugar free orange juice
1/4 cup chopped celery
1 tablespoon chopped parsley
1/2 teaspoon paprika
1/2 teaspoon ground red pepper
1/2 teaspoon cayenne pepper
1/2 teaspoon ground black pepper
2 cups croutons
1 - 4 to 5 pound beef prime rib roast

Soak croutons in orange juice in a large bowl. When soft add melted butter, onions, parsley, celery and spices. Mix well.

With a sharp knife slice roast into 1 and 1/2 inch thick slices. With a sharp knife make pockets in the prime rib roast slices along the fat side and in through the center of the meat. Stuff each pocket with stuffing. Close the opening with a wooden toothpick or bamboo skewer.

Sprinkle with salt and pepper to taste and sear over a very hot fire for about two minutes on each side. Cook on the indirect side of grill for about 8 minutes on each side or until meat reaches 135 degrees.

Kansas City Grilled Burger Bash

1/4 cup Worcestershire Sauce
1/4 cup melted butter or margarine
1/4 cup minced onions
1/4 teaspoon salt substitute
1/4 teaspoon celery seed
1 tablespoon chopped dill
1/2 teaspoon paprika
1/2 teaspoon ground red pepper
1/2 teaspoon cayenne pepper
1/2 teaspoon ground black pepper
8 Kansas City Steak Burgers

In a large bowl combine Worcestershire Sauce, butter and spices. Mix well and baste burgers for about 20 minutes.

Sprinkle with salt and pepper to taste and sear over a very hot fire for about two minutes on each side. Cook on the indirect side of grill for about 8 minutes on each side or until meat reaches 135 degrees.

We also recommend this recipe with Kansas City Steak Company Buffalo Burgers. Buffalo is a lean red meat that tastes just great with any of your favorite spicy ideas.

In Addition To Steak:

Barbeque Techniques And

Award-Winning Recipes

Now that you have had the opportunity to enjoy steaks that are the best in the universe, take time to delve further into the barbeque arts.

The recipes and techniques that follow are collected from the Kansas City Barbeque Inner Circle, whose membership includes contest winners, professionals in the business of barbeque, authors and creators of barbeque products and publications.

THE THREE DEGREES OF BARBEQUE

ABSOLUTE BARBEQUE employs the "Degree System," which groups recipes based on the amount of time involved during the barbecuing process. This arrangement makes it simple to select the pork, beef, poultry, lamb, sausage or seafood technique that best suits your time frame.

1ST DEGREE selections are generally completed in fifteen minutes to one hour. These are grilling techniques done over high heat. This quick-preparation section — "Punctual Perfection" — allows for all the sensory delights of true barbeque, yet accomplishes it in a short amount of time. A quickie unequalled.

2ND DEGREE creations — "Extended Excellence" — are affairs drawn out over more time, say two to four hours, where temperatures are lower and smoking is done on a covered unit. This section allows ample time to enjoy various other pleasures as smoke aroma pervades the senses.

3RD DEGREE efforts — "Lengthy Leisure" — are for those willing to put in a minimum of five hours in pursuit of the barbeque ideal. Some of these recipes, ambitious to the hilt, take upwards of fifteen hours, since large cuts require lots of slow-smoke time. But, as true barbeque warlords will attest, time spent barbecuing is a ritualistic reverie of the first magnitude, and worth every minute.

It is important to indicate here that the progression through 1st, 2nd and 3rd Degree recipes is simply a function of time. The recipes are not necessarily any more complex or difficult in later sections, but they will take longer to complete for Absolute Barbeque Perfection.

The Basics of Barbeque: Learning to Control the Elements

Cremated outside, raw inside.
Totally torched.
Dry and brittle.
Under-done and scary-looking.
Tastes like lighter fluid.
Looks like a penny loafer.

If lucky, you've somehow avoided all that's just been mentioned, but odds are you've had to endure backyard barbeque disasters when someone's good intentions fell well short of perfection. ABSOLUTE BARBEQUE is designed to help you avoid all of the mistakes listed above by making grilling and smoking simple and enjoyable.

Grilling and Smoking: Barbeque Techniques with Dramatic Differences

Grilling is done over high heat. Things cook rapidly, the unit is not covered, and true smoke flavor is a secondary consideration.

Smoking is done over low heat in a covered unit. Things cook more slowly, moisture is essential to the process, and smoke flavor is imparted.

The equipment used in the barbeque process can be varied, but all standard units, (Webers, various covered cookers, water smokers, gas grills, 55 gallon drums, etc.), can be used successfully with the techniques and recipes in ABSOLUTE BARBEQUE.

The Elements of Barbeque: Your Keys to Great Results

Controlling the four basic elements in barbecuing assures good results. The following is a typical scenario that outlines the proper way to 1) construct a fire, 2) control moisture, and 3) impart flavor. Element 4), time, becomes a product of the other three elements, as we will see.

Element One: Fire. Either wood or charcoal fires work well. Charcoal should be allowed to form a thin white ash before the cooking process begins.

If simply grilling, the coals should be spread out evenly with the grill three to five inches above the fire. Use of wood chips is optional.

When smoking, the fire should not be directly under the meat. Using indirect heat lowers the temperature and allows use of water pans, and drip pans. Set the cooking surface up as far from the fire as possible.

Element Two: Moisture. The retention and addition of moisture is a necessary component of the smoking art. This can be accomplished by basting the entré of choice, or using a water pan. Using soaked wood chunks or chips can help as well.

Element Three: Woods. The smoke flavor imparted by good, seasoned wood gives barbeque its uniqueness. Many chefs build their fires solely with favored woods, others place soaked chunks or chips on charcoal fires. Either method works well. Oak, Hickory, Apple, Cherry, Pecan — these and various other woods are all sworn to be the best, depending on the chef and what is being prepared.

Element Four: Time. This element can last minutes or hours depending on the control of the other three elements and the side and type of cut to be cooked. Thus, the suggested time for any recipe depends on the control of fire and moisture combined with the outdoor conditions.

Control of the elements requires some experimentation and magic. A proper fire, adequate moisture, flavorful wood — all will give good results. But other essentials aid in the preparation of mind-boggling barbeque, and that's what we'll discuss next.

Secrets Shared:
Easy Techniques to make
YOUR Barbeque Exquisite.

The following suggestions have been assembled from the combined knowledge of countless contest winners, product manufacturers, and barbeque titans whose sentiments generally flow along similar lines. In no particular order, these tips will allow for your complete and resounding barbeque success:

1) Familiarize yourself totally with your equipment.

2) Buy a real thermometer (don't trust any thermometer that comes on a smoker), and put it up by the top vents. When the temperature drops 20 to 25 degrees, add a handful of briquets and some wood.

3) Open bottom vents fully and control heat with top ones.

4) Smoking should be done between 200 to 225 degrees with light smoke and plenty of moisture. Place the water pan above the fire and away from the meat.

5) Make notes on what works and what needs to be tried the next time — don't trust your memory.

6) Use marinades or rubs (dry spices rubbed into the meat), whenever barbecuing.

7) Apply sauce only after the meat is off the grill, or have it on the side, or don't use it at all (if the marinade and/or rub has done its job properly).

8) Use a clean cooker every time — there's a definite difference in taste.

9) Use hickory sparingly — it can be overpowering and bitter.

10) Make sure any wood used is well seasoned.

11) Slow cooking is always preferred.

12) While "grocery store" charcoal is acceptable, lump hardwood charcoal (made from wood with a minimum of "fillers"), is preferable since it burns hotter, longer and cleaner.

13) Let anything that is destined for the grill or smoker reach room temperature first — do not start with cold meat.

14) Accessories: Many of the following items make successful barbeque easier and allow for more versatility.

Basting Brush

Tongs

Apron

Mitt

Wire Brush for Grill Cleaning

Charcoal Chimney for quick starting briquets

Spray Bottle for any Flare-ups

Water Pan(s)

Rotisserie

Rib Racks

Long Handled Spatula

Drip pan

Starters (solid/liquid/electric)

Symbols of Success

The Symbols of Success chart below depicts three elements critical to your barbeque success — time, temperature and smoke. The correct mix of these is found on each page of ABSOLUTE BARBEQUE; every recipe has its optimum formula illustrated.

As you can see, this recipe calls for three hours of cooking at a low, slow temperature, with slight smoke flavor.

This scientific application of the basic barbeque art is an "Inner Circle" first. A brief explanation of these elements follow.

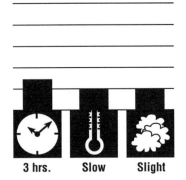

3 hrs.　　Slow　　Slight

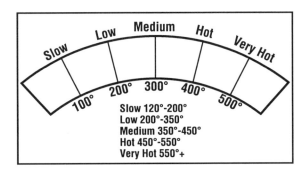

Slow 120°-200°
Low 200°-350°
Medium 350°-450°
Hot 450°-550°
Very Hot 550°+

Time

Time relates directly to the type and amount of product being cooked.

Temperature

Temperature varies with cooking time, with the hottest fires used for the shortest cooking, cooler fires for slow smoking. (See temperature gauge above.)

Smoke

Smoke permeates the meat over time, giving it the distinctive flavor of the type of wood being used.

The basic barbeque elements relate in ways that the Inner Circle further illustrates on the page opposite — Barbeque Mathematics. The Symbols of Success chart on each recipe page, as in the above illustration, is a "snapshot" of a point on the Barbeque Mathematics graph.

Barbeque Mathematics

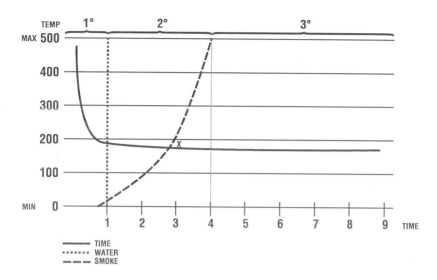

Do not be scared of this graph! Conceived in a barbeque-addled moment of transcendent inspiration, it shows how the elements of barbeque relate!

Time stretches out from left to right along the baseline, and corresponds to 1st, 2nd and 3rd degree sections in the book.

Temperature rises up the left side of the graph, and has been further illustrated using a more conventional temperature gauge (on the preceding page) for reference.

Smoke is imparted over time (notice how the temperature curve drops with time as the smoke curve rises).

The Inner Circle knows that each and every recipe contained in ABSOLUTE BARBECUE falls at some point within the graph above, containing just the right amount of each barbeque element. And with a Symbols of Success chart depicting an exact point from the Barbeque Mathematics graph, the proper mix of elements is insured on each recipe.

(The "X" on the graph shows the exact point for the Symbols of Success chart on the preceding page.)

With Barbeque Mathematics and Symbols of Success, the Inner Circle has explained the "scientific" elements of world-class barbeque. The recipes themselves, along with your own personal flair, provide the final magic that results in the sensory thrills of barbeque perfectly prepared.

All These Words Are Causing HUNGER! Let's Cook Something!

An Easy Smoked Sausage Technique To Get You Started:

1) Mound 20-25 hardwood charcoal briquets on one side of the fire grate in your smoker (or prepare a like amount in a charcoal chimney). Start the fire.

2) Allow sausage (let's try 5 pounds or so of mild to hot Italian, long and coiled) to reach room temperature.

3) When the coals are white, add pre-moistened wood chips or chunks (whatever type you choose). Don't spread the coals out as you would for grilling: leave it pretty well piled up on one side so that you can place the meat opposite, not above, the fire. Add a water pan, if desired.

4) Place the sausage on the grill away from the fire, have the bottom vents wide open, close the lid.

5) Monitor the temperature in the smoker and adjust it to 200-220 degrees by opening/closing the top-side vents. Once this temperature is reached, the only reason to open the lid is to add more briquets/wood (if temperature drops 20-25 degrees). Some smoke should be wafting out of the unit at all times.

6) Continue to monitor the temperature, turn the sausage a time or two, add fuel if necessary. And an hour to an hour and a half later, pull it out, add some sauce if you feel like it, and have a smoked sausage feast!

This same technique would work for chicken pieces (you might want to marinate the chicken and baste during smoking), or a small pork tenderloin (with which you might want to use a good basic rub).

Use your imagination with woods, marinades, rubs and spices, all of which are outlined in the recipes to follow.

ABSOLUTE BARBEQUE

We all know the feeling. That wonderful aroma has been in the air for just long enough. The conversation has been good, the beverages refreshing. But an expectant nerve twitch has been egged on, hour upon hour, by the anticipation, the hankering, for what's right over there in the smoker.

The host has been cordial, but its getting hard to wait another minute because the entire atmosphere, delicately laced with smoke and comraderie, has made everyone's palate insistent and demanding, desirous of that foremost expression of smoke art — barbeque expertly prepared, bursting with flavor and sensual delight.

The entire scenario is making everyone WILD ABOUT BARBEQUE!!!

Ravenous, insatiable guests about to pounce! Unchecked, this is what it comes to: *Adults unable to help themselves. The allure of the smoke, the call of the "Q." Passion in need of an outlet...*

ABSOLUTE BARBEQUE is not an overstatement. Anyone fortunate enough to have partaken of truly transcendental smoked goods has been marked for life, and what forms does this wildness take? Why so wild about ABSOLUTE BARBEQUE?

Because barbeque is versatile.

The various items in this tome range from simple to complex. The settings for such culinary delights can be casual or elegant. The audience for these dishes is unbounded by age, background or social status. Barbeque appeals to everyone.

Because barbeque is functional.

The techniques used herein enable the user to create exquisite results from anything. Originally conceived as a way to "make do" with whatever was available, barbeque became an art form as marinades, rubs, spices and smoke enhanced any and all cuts of meat.

Because barbeque is an event.

Without barbeque, how could one even relate to the Fourth of July? Would Memorial Day, Father's Day and Labor Day approximate their fond hold on our imaginations were it not for barbeque? Indeed, does not the ritual and ceremony involved in the bond of barbeque make it a uniting force for family and friends? Such is the strength of "Q."

Because barbeque is personal.

True devotees of the grill are as proud of their efforts as any artist or craftsman. The long hours spent tending fires are borne out of a sense of passion for their creations. The satisfaction experienced by chef and guest are bonds that are not to be taken lightly.

Because barbeque is AMERICAN.

No form of cooking is so identifiably American as the backyard barbeque. Nothing else even comes close.

ABSOLUTE BARBEQUE.

In many ways an understatement, our appreciation for this heart-felt and uniquely American art form stems from a belief that barbecuing is an ideal way to spend time with friends and family, to explore new techniques in an exceptionally personal form of expression, and to enjoy the myriad aromas, textures and flavors inherent in barbeque's rich and varied world.

Beginnings of the Perfect BBQ

APPETIZERS

Chinese Fire Drill Beef Strips

1 pound beef fillet
1/2 cup soy sauce
1 clove garlic (pressed)
1 tsp. ginger (ground)

Cut fillet or tenderloin into thin strips. Mix all other ingredients and pour over beef strips. Let marinate for about one hour. Thread the beef on small bamboo skewers and grill one minute on each side. Baste with remaining marinade after turning.

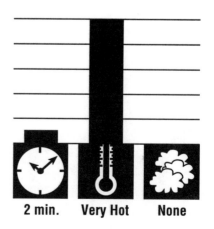

2 min.   Very Hot   None

Fiesta Livers

1 pound chicken livers
1 cup Madeira
1 tbsp. garlic salt
bacon strips
salt and pepper
butter or margarine

Marinate livers for two hours in a mixture of Madeira, garlic, salt and pepper. Saute livers in butter for several minutes and allow to cool. Wrap each liver in a bacon strip, threading four livers to bamboo skewer. Grill until bacon is crisp, about six minutes.

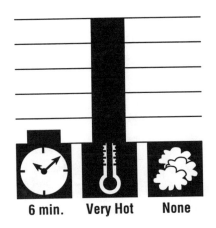

6 min.   Very Hot   None

Backyard Grilled Spiced Shrimp

1 pound shrimp
1 stick butter or margarine
2 tbsp. Backyard BBQ & Grill Seasoning[1]
1 can beer

Peel and clean shrimp, place five to six pieces on well soaked bamboo skewers. Melt butter and stir in Backyard BBQ & Grill Seasoning. A generic spiced rub can be substituted. Brush shrimp with spiced butter and grill over hot coals until pink, about five to seven minutes. Continue to brush with butter. If flames should erupt, douse with beer and apply more butter.

[1]BBQ & Grill Seasoning — If unavailable in your area, you can create your own mixture. Combine 1 part paprika, 1 part ground black pepper, and 1 part salt. Mix a large batch and use as needed with your favorite backyard recipes.

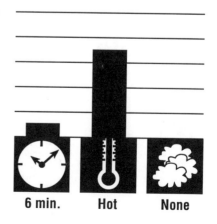

6 min.   Hot   None

Grilled Mussels Au Shroom

24 large mussels
24 mushroom caps
24 2 inch strips of bacon
1 cup crushed bread crumbs
1/2 cup flour
1/4 cup minced parsley

1/2 cup olive oil
2 eggs (beaten)
1 cup white wine
1 cup water
1 tbsp. butter or margarine
2 cloves garlic (pressed)

Thoroughly clean mussels and steam in a covered saucepan until they open. Remove the shell and pat dry. Combine the white wine, water and butter, bring to a boil, and saute mushroom caps for two to three minutes. Thread the mussels, mushrooms and bacon on bamboo skewers, coat with flour, dip in egg, then coat with bread crumbs. Grill over a hot fire, basting with olive oil, parsley and garlic. Turn and baste for about five minutes on each side or until toasted.

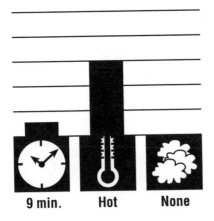

9 min.   Hot   None

Waddle's Magic Meatballs

1 pound ground sirloin
1 egg
Pimento stuffed green olives
Salt and Pepper
Garlic powder
Olive oil
Parsley flakes

Combine ground sirloin, egg, garlic, salt and pepper. Shape mixture around each olive to make a meatball twice the size of the olive. Brush meatballs with olive oil and roll in parsley. Place four meatballs on well soaked bamboo skewers and grill until brown.

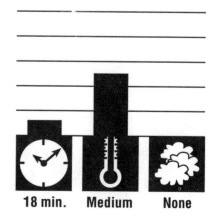

18 min.   Medium   None

Mama's Italian Sausage Poppers

1/2 pound Italian sausage
1/2 pound proscuito ham
1/2 pound hard salami
1/2 pound lean bacon strips
1/4 cup parsley flakes
1 tsp. crushed oregano
1/4 cup minced onion
1 tbsp. lemon juice

Combine sausage, ham and salami in a food processor. Chop on fine. Add parsley, oregano, onion and lemon juice. Mix thoroughly. Form one-inch balls with the mixture and wrap with bacon strips. Place three balls on each bamboo skewer and grill until bacon is crisp. Make sure bamboo skewers are well soaked in water before grilling.

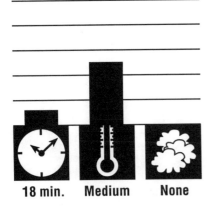

18 min.   Medium   None

Father's Fourth of July Salmon

**1 large whole salmon
1 cup Backyard Lemon Butter Seasoning[2]
2 cups Italian Dressing
1/2 cup olive oil**

In a large bowl, mix Lemon Butter and Italian Dressing. Allow to sit for about fifteen minutes. Take salmon, fresh from market, and rub with olive oil, inside and out. Generously spread lemon butter mixture on salmon, inside and out. Place salmon on heavy duty aluminum foil, or grill rack, and smoke for about ten minutes per pound. A blend of hickory and apple woods will lend great flavor to this dish. Leave the skin on for cooking, and peel back for serving. Cover with more lemon butter sauce as a garnish.

[2]Backyard Lemon Butter Seasoning — If unavailable in your area, you can create your own mixture. Combine 1/4 cup lemon juice, 1/4 cup melted butter, 1 tsp. ground dill, and 1 tsp. garlic salt. Mix a large batch and use as needed with your favorite backyard recipes.

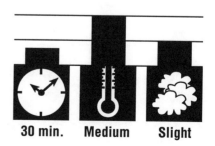

30 min.   Medium   Slight

Bob E.'s Smoked Stuffed Artichokes

4 large artichokes
2 tbsp. butter or margarine
4 tbsp. olive oil
1/4 cup chopped onion
1/4 cup chopped celery
1/2 cup chopped zucchini
1 clove garlic, pressed

1/4 cup lemon juice
1/4 cup shredded mozzarella cheese
1 tbsp. ground black pepper
1 tsp. salt
1/4 cup bread crumbs

Cook artichokes in boiling salted water for thirty minutes. Remove and drain water. Remove outer leaves and spoon out center. Place artichoke hearts, onion, celery, zucchini and garlic in a saucepan with olive oil and butter. Simmer until mixture is softened. Place mixture in a food processor and puree. Combine with remaining ingredients, stir, and stuff into artichoke shells. Smoke over apple wood fire for about thirty minutes.

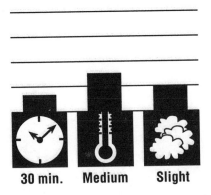

30 min.   Medium   Slight

Rick's Hot Wings

5 pounds chicken wings
1 pound butter or margarine
1/2 cup Backyard BBQ & Grill Seasoning[3]
1/2 cup white vinegar
1/4 cup Louisiana Hot Sauce
1 tbsp. Tabasco Sauce

Clean wings, place in a clean trash bag. Pour vinegar over wings, hold bag tightly closed and shake. Pour BBQ & Grill Seasoning in bag and shake again. Place wings on grill and smoke for about twenty minutes. In a sauce pan, melt butter and add tabasco and hot sauce. Stir well, then brush half of mixture over wings. Cook for another five to ten minutes. Place wings on large platter, pour remainder of sauce mixture over and serve.

[3]BBQ & Grill Seasoning — If unavailable in your area, you can create your own mixture. Combine 1 part paprika, 1 part ground black pepper, and 1 part salt. Mix a large batch and use as needed with your favorite backyard recipes.

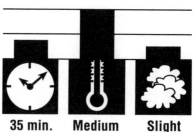

35 min.   Medium   Slight

Spicy Smoked Skins

4 large baked potatoes
1 cup cheddar cheese
1/2 cup sour cream
1/2 cup butter or margarine
1 tsp. garlic powder
1 tsp, chili powder
1 tsp. ground black pepper
1 tsp. salt

Slice baked potatoes in half. Spoon out pulp into a mixing bowl, leaving about a quarter of an inch of potato on the skin. Add butter, sour cream and spices to the potato and mix well. Stir in half of the cheddar cheese. Place the skins on aluminum foil or grill rack, and smoke for about thirty minute. Remove from grill and fill with potato mixture. Top with remainder of cheddar cheese and return to smoker for an additional thirty minutes, or until cheese is melted. Cut into bite size pieces and serve hot.

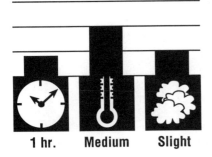

1 hr.   Medium   Slight

Lemon Grilled Veggies

1 pound broccoli
1/2 pound cauliflower
1/2 pound carrots
1/2 pound potatoes
2 cloves garlic

1 cup olive oil
2 tsp. salt
2 tsp. pepper
1 large lemon
1 tbsp. lemon juice

Cut broccoli and cauliflower into spears. Slice potatoes into wedges and carrots into strips. Mix garlic, oil, salt and pepper and allow to set for 15 minutes. Boil veggies in a large pot for about 3 minutes. Place on grill rack away from fire and baste with oil mixture. Slice lemon and add to grill rack. Pour lemon juice over everything. Grill until potatoes are brown and others tender, about one hour.

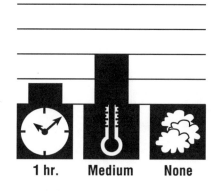

1 hr.   Medium   None

Punctual
Perfection

1ST DEGREE
SPECIALTIES

Absolute Grilled Shrimp

1-1/2 lbs. large shrimp
8 tbsp. melted butter (1 stick)
1/2 tsp. garlic powder
1 tbs. paprika
1/2 tsp. celery salt
1/2 tsp dry mustard
1 tbsp. sugar
1/2 tsp. ground sage
1/2 tsp. onion salt

Prepare shrimp — peel and devein, leaving tail on. Melt butter and stir in seasonings. Place shrimp in a flat dish and stir in seasonings. Place shrimp in a flat dish, cover with marinade and refrigerate for one hour. Place shrimp on skewers or grill rack. Grill for about 3 to 4 minutes, turn and grill for another 2 minutes. Pour marinade over shrimp while cooking.

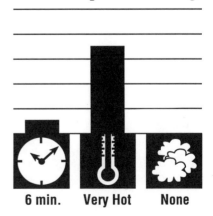

6 min.   Very Hot   None

Grilled Haddock

4, 1 1/4" haddock steaks
1/3 cup butter or margarine
1/2 tsp. salt
1/2 tsp. pepper
1/2 cup flour

Sprinkle the steaks with salt and pepper, then dust with flour. Brush with melted butter. Place fish on grill rack over a medium fire for eight minutes. Brush with butter while cooking. Fish will "flake" when poked with fork when done, about another four minutes. Serve with fresh lemon halves and melted butter.

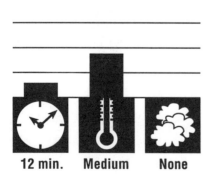

12 min.   Medium   None

Barbequed Fajitas

2 pound flank steak
1/4 cup soy sauce
1/8 cup Backyard BBQ & Grill Seasoning[4]
1/4 cup white vinegar
1/4 cup white wine
2 green bell peppers
1 large onion
2 red bell pepper
1/2 cup black olives

Combine soy sauce, Backyard BBQ & Grill Seasoning, vinegar, and white wine. Soak steak in mixture for about fifteen minutes. Place steak on grill, and cook for about seven to eight minutes on each side. Place marinade mixture in a disposable foil pan, slice vegetables and place in mixture. Place pan on grill while steak is cooking. Vegetables will saute in marinade as steak cooks. Serve with flour tortillas.

[4]BBQ & Grill Seasoning — If unavailable in your area, you can create your own mixture. Combine 1 part paprika, 1 part ground black pepper, and 1 part salt. Mix a large batch and use as needed with your favorite backyard recipes.

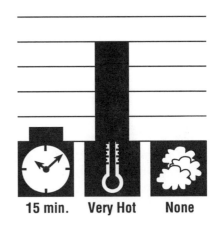

15 min.   Very Hot   None

Great White on the Grill

2 shark steaks
2 lemons
1 onion
2 pieces aluminum foil
1 tbsp. cracked black pepper
1 tbsp. salt
2 tbsp. butter or margarine

Grease foil sheets with butter and place shark on foil. Slice onions and lemons and place half on each piece of shark. Sprinkle with salt and pepper. Seal foil tightly and place on grill for about ten minutes per pound. Remove from grill and let stand for about five minutes. Carefully open foil, shark will be steaming. Place on a platter, garnish with lemons and butter.

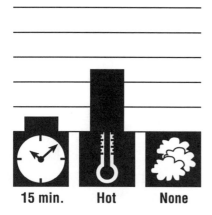

15 min.   Hot   None

Spicy Grilled Trout

4 trout, heads removed
1/3 cup olive oil
1/3 cup wine vinegar
1 tsp. garlic salt
1 tsp. black pepper
1 tsp. paprika
1 tsp. cayenne pepper
1 tsp. mustard powder
1 tsp. chile pepper
1/4 cup water

Clean and pat dry fish. Mix remaining ingredients in a small sauce pan and bring to a boil. Place fish on a grill rack over hot coals and brush with sauce mixture. Cook for about fifteen minutes, turn and re-brush with sauce often.

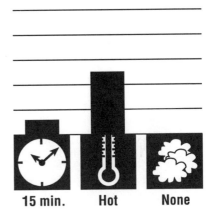

15 min.   Hot   None

Bob E.'s Chicken Steaks

4 boneless chicken breasts
1/4 cup butter or margarine
1/8 cup lemon juice
1/2 tsp. marjoram
1/2 tsp. paprika
1/2 tsp. salt

Melt butter and combine with salt, lemon juice and marjoram. Brush chicken with sauce, and place on grill rack over hot coals, grill ten minutes, turn and grill for five to six more minutes. Sprinkle with paprika. Serve with fresh lemon halves.

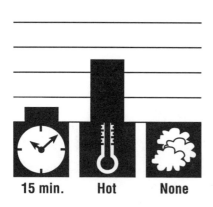

15 min.   Hot   None

Kelsey's Grilled Catfish

4 catfish
1/2 cup red wine vinegar
1 tbsp. oregano
1 tbsp. salt
1 tbsp. coarse ground pepper
1/2 cup flour

Clean and gut catfish. Rub down with vinegar, inside and out. Combine remaining ingredients in a small bowl. Dust cavity with the seasoned flour. Grill for about seven minutes with skin side down, away from fire. When skin pulls back, grill for about another seven minutes. Cook for about a total of 15 minutes, using indirect method.

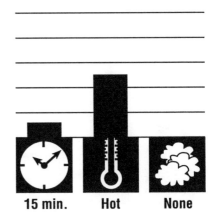

15 min.   Hot   None

Roughy on the Rough

3 pounds orange roughy
1/4 cup minced onion
1/4 cup minced parsley
1 tsp. salt
1 tsp. ground black pepper
4 strips lean bacon
1 lemon
1 stick butter or margarine

Wash and pat dry roughy. Cut a twelve inch square of aluminum foil for each piece of roughy, and lightly butter each square. Place roughy on the foil and sprinkle with onion, parsley, salt and pepper. Place a half strip of bacon on each piece of roughy and fold over the foil. Seal tightly. Set the foil packages directly onto white hot coals. Cook for about fifteen minutes, turning every five minutes. Serve with fresh lemon wedges.

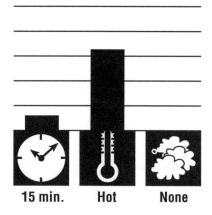

15 min.   Hot   None

Randy's Bootz Steak

4 ribeye steaks
2 cups red wine
2 tbsp. oregano
2 tbsp. salt
2 tbsp. coarse black pepper
1/2 cup raspberry preserves
1 cup barbeque sauce
1 tsp. tabasco sauce

Marinate steaks for about two hours in wine and spices. Grill over hot fire for about seven minutes on each side. Mix raspberry preserves with barbeque sauce. Add tabasco sauce and pour over steaks.

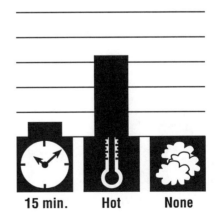

15 min.   Hot   None

Mac's Hot Buttered Swordfish

4 Swordfish steaks
2 lemons
1 stick butter or margarine
1 clove garlic
2 tbsp. anchovy paste

1 tsp. salt
2 tsp. ground black pepper
1 tsp. ground paprika
1 tsp. ground red pepper
1 tsp. ground white pepper

Place swordfish on aluminum foil and sprinkle with salt and pepper. Melt butter in a sauce pan, and add juice from the lemons, anchovy paste and garlic. Baste swordfish generously, and grill for ten to fifteen minutes. Turn at least once, and continue to baste with butter mixture. Remove from grill and top with paprika, red and white peppers.

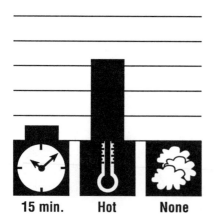

15 min.   Hot   None

Greek BBQ Ke-Bobs

2 pounds lamb steak, cubed
1/4 cup olive oil
1/2 cup lemon juice
1 tbsp. cracked black pepper
1 tbsp. salt
1 tbsp. ground dill
12 1-inch cubes green pepper
12 small onions
12 cherry tomatoes

Trim fat off lamb and marinate in olive oil, lemon juice, salt, pepper and dill. Let stand for twenty to thirty minutes. Soak vegetables in boiling water for about three minutes. Thread lamb and vegetables onto skewers and grill for about ten to fifteen minutes. Turn frequently, and baste with marinade while grilling.

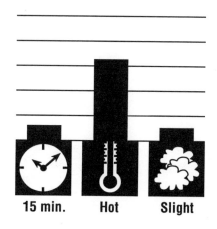

15 min.   Hot   Slight

Wild Bill's Sizzl'n Sirloin

4, 12 ounce sirloin steaks
2 cups Big Bill's Favorite Steak Marinade[5]
1 tbsp. cracked black pepper
1 tsp. garlic powder

Marinate steaks for about thirty minutes. Sear each side for about thirty seconds over hot fire. Move steaks to cool side of grill, cover and cook for seven minutes. Flip, pour left over marinade over steaks and cook for another seven minutes. Should produce the perfect medium-rare steak.

[5]Big Bill's Favorite Steak Marinade — The recipe for this fabulous creation can be found on page 129. You can also use your own favorite steak marinade, but try Big Bill's. It's out of this world.

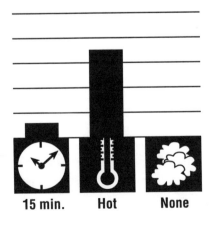

15 min.   **Hot**   **None**

Smoked Fish Steaks

2 pounds fresh fish steaks
1/2 cup soy sauce
1/8 cup olive oil
1 clove garlic, chopped
1/4 tsp. ginger, ground
1/4 cup onion, chopped

Combine soy sauce, oil, garlic, onions and ginger. Set aside for fifteen minutes. Place fish in a large bowl and cover with the marinade. Allow to stand for one hour, then drain. Place fish on grill rack, and grill over hickory wood fire for fifteen to twenty minutes. Turn often and baste with remaining marinade.

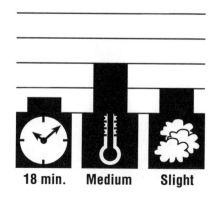

18 min.   Medium   Slight

Too Cool T-Bone

2 T-Bone Steaks
1 cup white wine
1/2 cup butter or margarine
1 cup sliced mushrooms
2 cloves garlic
1 tsp. salt
1 tsp. cracked black pepper
2 tbsp. Italian Dressing

Bring steaks to room temperature, then brush with Italian Dressing. Sear on hot grill for about one minute on each side. Remove to cool side of grill, cover and cook for seven minutes. Flip, then cook for 6 minutes. After searing and covering grill, melt butter, add mushrooms and garlic. Saute for about two to three minutes, add wine, salt and pepper and saute until steaks are done. Pour mushroom and butter mixture over steaks and serve.

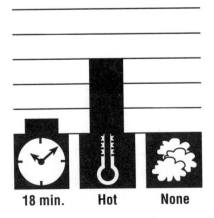

18 min.   Hot   None

Grilled Minute Steak

2 pounds minute steak
1 cup flour
1 tbsp. ground black pepper
1 tsp. cayenne pepper
1 tsp. ground red pepper
1 tsp. paprika
1 tbsp. salt
2 eggs

Mix flour and spices in a large flat dish. Scramble eggs in another flat dish. Tenderize steak with a large meat hammer. Beat very thin. Dip steaks in egg bath, then in spiced flour. Generously coat both sides. Place on hot grill, cook flipping frequently until crust is golden brown. Serve with a spicy sweet barbecue sauce.

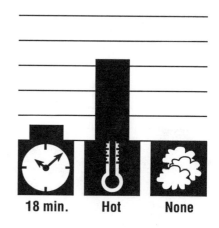

18 min.   Hot   None

Ricky's Steak Flambe

1 two-inch sirloin steak
1/2 cup melted butter
1 tbsp. ground black pepper
1 tsp. salt
1/4 cup Tanqueray Gin

Rub steak with salt and pepper. Sear on each side over a hot fire for about one minute. Move steak to cool side of grill, cover and cook for about ten minutes. Turn and cook for about seven more minutes. Melt butter in a sauce pan, stir in Tanqueray and warm mixture slowly. Place steak on a warm, metal serving tray. Ignite butter sauce and pour over steak. Present at table and slice while still flaming.

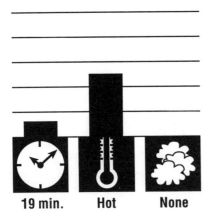

19 min.   Hot   None

Ron & Dave's Mexican Jumping Steak

4, 1-inch sirloin steaks
1 tbsp. cumin
1 tbsp. cayenne pepper
1 tbsp. habanero pepper sauce
1 tbsp. tabasco sauce
1 tbsp. white pepper
1/4 cup water
1/4 cup white vinegar

Combine spices with vinegar and water. Marinate steaks in mixture for about thirty minutes. Grill to your liking. Pour marinade on steaks while cooking.

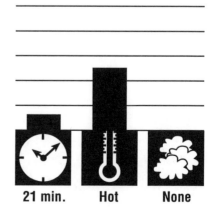

21 min.   Hot   None

Mad Dog's Center Cut Sirloin

2, 1 1/2 inch Center Cut Sirloin
1/8 cup No Misteaks Marinade[6]
2 tbsp. white vinegar
1 cup hot water
2 tbsp. No Misteaks Seasoning[7]

Combine water, vinegar and steak marinade. Mix well and let stand for fifteen minutes. Bring steaks to room temperature, then pour marinade over steaks and marinate for fifteen minutes. Place steaks on a hot grill and sear for about two minutes on each side. Move steaks to cool side of grill and pour marinade on steak. Cover grill and allow to cook for seven minutes, flip and cook for seven more minutes for a perfect medium-rare steak. Top with steak seasoning and serve.

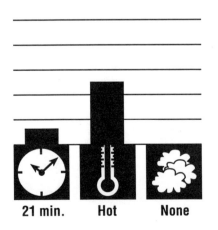

21 min.   Hot   None

[6]No Misteaks Marinade — If unavailable in your area, you can create your own mixture. Combine 1 part B-V Beef Broth, and 1 part Lea & Perrin Sauce. Mix a large batch and use as needed with your favorite backyard recipes.

[7]No Misteaks Seasoning — If unavailable in your area, you can create your own mixture. Combine 1/2 tsp. garlic powder, 1/2 tsp. ground onion powder, 1 tsp. ground black pepper, and 1/2 tsp. salt. Mix a large batch and use as needed with your favorite backyard recipes.

Grilled Stuffed Flank Steak

2 pounds flank steak	1 tsp. black pepper
4 tbsp. butter or margarine	1 tsp. mustard powder
1/2 cup minced mushrooms	1/4 cup white wine
1 tsp. garlic powder	1/2 cup minced onion

Trim flank steak to remove any fat. Cut a pocket into the steak, but keep the opening as narrow as possible. Sprinkle salt and pepper on the steak and set aside. In a skillet, combine wine, butter, mustard, salt and pepper. Heat until butter melts, then add mushrooms and saute for two minutes. Add onion and stir. Pour off excess liquid for use as a baste. Stuff mixture into steak and grill over a hot fire for about five minutes on each side. If stuffing comes out of opening, secure with a wet bamboo skewer before grilling. Pour baste on steak after turning.

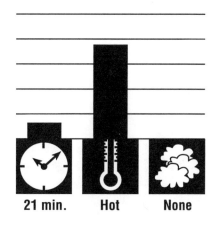

21 min.   Hot   None

Absolute Lobster Tails

4 lobster tails (7-8 oz.)
1/2 cup melted butter
   or margarine
2 tbsp. dry white wine
1/2 tsp. garlic powder
1 tbsp. paprika

1/2 tsp. celery salt
1/2 tsp. dry mustard
1 tbsp. sugar
1/2 tsp. ground sage
1/2 tsp. onion salt
4 lemon wedges

Using a sharp knife, cut through top membrane and remove. Slightly loosen meat from the shell, leaving tail connected. Combine butter, wine and spices in a small bowl. Stir well and brush over lobster meat. Place lobster tails, shell side down, on grill rack or foil, away from fire. Grill on low fire for about 30 minutes or until meat is opaque. Serve immediately with lemon wedges and melted butter.

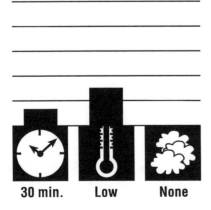

30 min.   Low   None

George's Championship Sausage

2 pounds bulk Italian sausage
1/8 cup dry rub
2 tbsp. onion flakes
2 tbsp. worcestershire sauce
1 cup barbecue sauce

Combine ingredients in a mixing bowl, working spices in with sausage. Use your favorite dry rub…George's is a secret. Form sausage into patties and smoke over a hickory fire for about 30 minutes. Pour your favorite barbecue sauce on (George's is a secret too!).

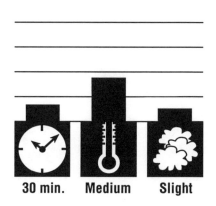

30 min.   Medium   Slight

The Kansas City Strip

4 Kansas City Strip Steaks
4 tsp. ground black pepper
2 tsp. salt
2 tsp. garlic powder
1/4 cup worcestershire sauce
4 tbsp. butter or margarine

Bring steaks to room temperature. Place in a flat dish and pour on worcestershire sauce. Sprinkle on salt, pepper and garlic. Allow to marinate for about fifteen minutes. Sear steaks for about one minute per side on a hot grill. Move steaks to cool side of grill, cook covered for seven minutes, flip and cook covered for five minutes. Place butter on each steak. Cover and cook for about one more minute.

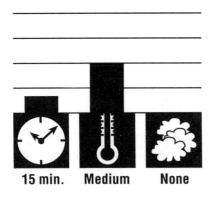

15 min.   Medium   None

Rick's Champion Rack of Lamb

6 rib rack of lamb
1 cup Italian Dressing
1/2 cup Backyard Lemon Butter Seasoning[8]
1 tsp. salt
1 tsp. cracked black pepper

Combine lemon butter and Italian dressing. Allow to stand for fifteen to twenty minutes. Salt and pepper lamb and place on grill for fifteen minutes. Slice rack, top each medallion with lemon butter mixture. Return to grill for about ten minutes.

[8]Backyard Lemon Butter Seasoning — If unavailable in your area, you can create your own mixture. Combine 1/4 cup lemon juice, 1/4 cup melted butter, 1 tsp. ground dill, and 1 tsp. garlic salt. Mix a large batch and use as needed with your favorite backyard recipes.

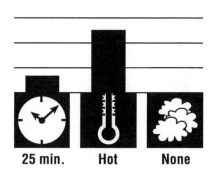

| 25 min. | Hot | None |

Maddog Pork Steaks

6 1-inch pork steaks
6 tbsp. white vinegar
6 tbsp. Backyard BBQ & Grill Seasoning[9]
6 tbsp. soy sauce

Rub steaks with vinegar and soy sauce. Soak both sides, then sprinkle with Backyard BBQ & Grill Seasoning. Grill for about fifteen minutes on each side. For a slightly spicy taste, allow steaks to marinate for several hours before grilling.

[9]BBQ & Grill Seasoning — If unavailable in your area, you can create your own mixture. Combine 1 part paprika, 1 part ground black pepper, and 1 part salt. Mix a large batch and use as needed with your favorite backyard recipes.

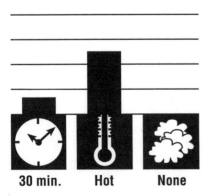

30 min.　　Hot　　None

Margarita's Chicken

8 boneless chicken breasts
1/2 cup olive oil
1/4 cup lemon juice
1 tbsp. dill
1/2 cup butter or margarine
1 tsp. cumin
1 tsp. salt
1 tsp. ground red pepper
1 clove garlic, pressed

Coat breasts with olive oil and lemon juice. Sprinkle on dill, cumin, salt and red pepper. Melt butter and add garlic. Pour garlic butter over breasts and grill for ten to fifteen minutes per side over a hot fire.

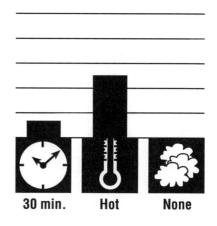

30 min.   Hot   None

Grilled Beer Brats

8 bratwurst
2 bottles dark german beer
1 clove garlic, pressed

Place brats, beer and garlic in a disposable foil pan over a hot grill. Bring to a boil. Remove brats, split and grill over hot coals about three minutes per side. Turn frequently.

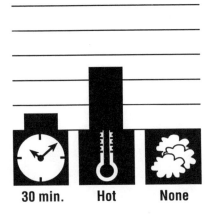

30 min.   Hot   None

Cap'n Happy's Lemon Grilled Bass

1 whole bass
1/4 cup lemon juice
1/4 cup butter or margarine
2 tbsp. chopped dill
salt and pepper

Split the bass and rub with lemon juice. Brush both sides of bass with melted butter and sprinkle with salt and pepper. Place bass on grill rack, skin side up, and grill for about 10 minutes per pound. Baste with a mixture of lemon juice, butter and dill. Remove skin after grilling to retain moisture.

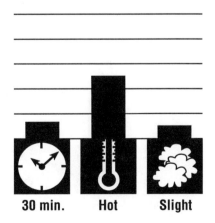

30 min.   Hot   Slight

Ricky's Porked Chops

4 pork chops, 1 1/2 inch
1 clove garlic, pressed
1/4 cup butter or margarine
1/4 cup orange juice
1 onion, chopped
1 tbsp. marjoram
1 cup bread crumbs
1 tbsp. salt
1 tbsp. ground black pepper

Trim chops and cut a pocket into the side. Melt butter. Combine remaining ingredients in a mixing bowl, stir well and stuff into chops. Grill over mesquite fire for thirty minutes. Brush with butter and turn frequently.

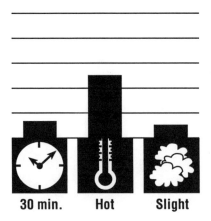

30 min.   Hot   Slight

Jay and David's Award Winning Mustard Steak

2 pound center cut sirloin
1/4 cup prepared yellow mustard
1/4 cup worcestershire sauce
1 tsp. cracked black pepper

Place steak in a flat dish and bring to room temperature. Spoon mustard onto steak and rub with fingers. Add worcestershire sauce and continue to rub until both sides of steak are covered with a tan mixture. Sprinkle generously with pepper. Allow to sit for about thirty minutes. Grill to your liking.

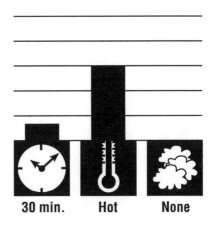

30 min.   Hot   None

Bidnessmen's Beef Burgers

2 pounds ground chuck
1/4 cup worcestershire sauce
1 tsp. garlic powder
1 tbsp. black pepper
1/4 cup minced onion
1/4 cup minced green pepper
2 tbsp. Backyard BBQ & Grill Seasoning[10]
2 tsp. No Misteaks Seasoning[11]

In a large bowl, combine ground chuck, worcestershire sauce, garlic, black pepper, minced onion and green peppers. Mix thoroughly, then form mixture into eight equal balls. Flatten into patties, top with Backyard BBQ & Grill Seasoning and Steak Seasoning. Grill over hot fire to your liking.

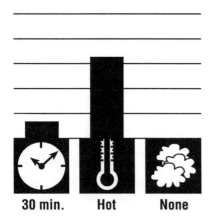

30 min.   Hot   None

[10]BBQ & Grill Seasoning — If unavailable in your area, you can create your own mixture. Combine 1 part paprika, 1 part ground black pepper, and 1 part salt. Mix a large batch and use as needed with your favorite backyard recipes.

[11]No Misteaks Seasoning — If unavailable in your area, you can create your own mixture. Combine 1/2 tsp. garlic powder, 1/2 tsp. ground onion powder, 1 tsp. ground black pepper, and 1/2 tsp. salt. Mix a large batch and use as needed with your favorite backyard recipes.

Zesty Sir-Lime Burgers

2 pounds ground sirloin
1/4 cup lime juice
1 tbsp. sugar
1 tbsp. zest of lime
1 clove garlic, pressed
1 egg

Combine ingredients in a bowl and mix well. Form into six to eight patties and grill to your liking.

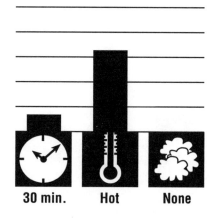

30 min.   Hot   None

Grilled Breast of Lamb

2-1/2 pound lamb breast
1 large onion
2 whole cloves garlic, pressed
1/2 cup olive oil
1 cup red wine
1 tbsp. cracked black pepper
1 tsp. salt
1 tsp. ground rosemary
1 tsp. ground thyme

Trim fat from lamb and place in a flat dish. Combine remaining ingredients in a small bowl, stir well and pour over lamb. Marinate in refrigerator overnight. Drain and grill over apple wood for about twenty minutes on each side. Baste with marinade. Lamb will be done when edges start to get brown and crispy.

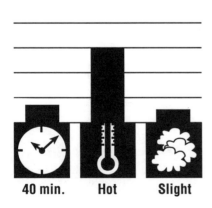

40 min.   Hot   Slight

Riley Dog's Lemon & Butter Breasts

8 split breasts
1 cup fresh lemon juice
8 tbsp. butter or margarine
8 tsp. lemon pepper

Place breasts on a cookie sheet. Make a slit in the thickest part of the breast, and stuff with one tablespoon of butter for each breast. Pour lemon juice on chicken, then sprinkle with lemon pepper. Grill over hickory fire for about fifty minutes to an hour. Baste with lemon juice every twenty minutes.

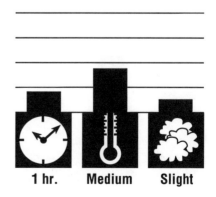

1 hr.   Medium   Slight

Barbie's Grilled Chick Chick

3 pounds chicken breast
3/4 cup white wine
1/4 cup water
1 onion
black pepper in mill
1 tsp. salt

1/4 pound butter
1/2 cup flour
1 tbsp. paprika
1 tbsp. red pepper
1 tbsp. white pepper

Clean, skin and bone chicken. Cut into bite size pieces. Combine wine, water, onion, 1 tsp. salt, and freshly ground pepper in a sauce pan. Simmer chicken in mixture for about 15 minutes. Combine flour and remaining dry ingredients, mix and set aside. Allow chicken to cool in sauce pan. Drain and roll chicken in the flour mixture. Brush with melted butter, place on grill rack and grill over a medium hickory fire until brown.

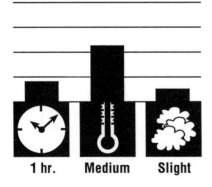

1 hr.   Medium   Slight

Bob E.'s Pork Key-Bobs

2 pounds pork roast
1/4 cup orange juice
1/4 cup lemon juice
1/2 cup olive oil
1/4 tsp. salt
1/2 tsp. black pepper

1 clove garlic
2 green bell peppers
2 red bell peppers
1 jar large cocktail onions
1 pound cherry tomatoes

Cut pork roast into inch and a half cubes and place on wet bamboo skewers. Combine remaining ingredients in a small bowl, and allow to sit for about fifteen minutes. Brush mixture on pork and place Key-Bobs on a grill rack and grill for about five minutes. Turn skewers and brush with marinade frequently. Remove from hot side of grill and smoke over hickory wood for about one hour. Cut peppers into cubes and place on skewers with onions and tomatoes. Smoke with pork until all are done.

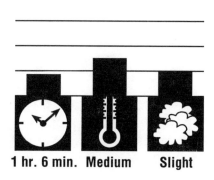

1 hr. 6 min.   Medium   Slight

Cheater's Ribs

2 slabs pork ribs
2 cups water
1/2 cup McCormick American Whiskey
2 tbsp. dry rub
1/2 cup white vinegar
1 crock pot

Cut slabs in half or thirds so that they fit in the crock pot. Sprinkle with dry rub, and place in crock pot. Pour in water. Be careful not to remove spice from ribs. Do the same with whiskey and vinegar. Place lid on crock pot, set for low heat and go to work. After you get home, light grill, let coals blaze until eighty percent ashed. Add a hand full of hickory chips to charcoal. Place ribs on grill and smoke for about one hour. Your friends will think you spent the whole day at home smoking!

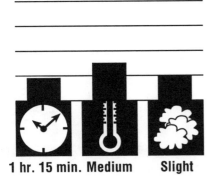

1 hr. 15 min.   Medium   Slight

Spicy Cheap-Skate Steak

4 lbs. round steak
1/4 cup worcestershire sauce
1/4 cup beef bouillon
1/4 cup yellow mustard
1/8 cup olive oil
1/8 cup white vinegar
1 tsp. salt
1 tbsp. ground black pepper

Mix all ingredients in a large sealable bag. Add round steak and shake well. Refrigerate for several hours. Sear meat over a hot fire for about 30 seconds on each side. Move to cool side of grill and cook for about an hour and 15 minutes. Baste and turn often.

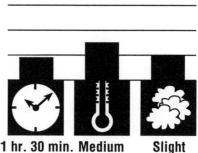

1 hr. 30 min. Medium Slight

Extended Excellence

2ND DEGREE SPECIALTIES

Down & Dirty Ribs

4 slabs, large
1/4 cup worcestershire sauce
1/2 cup brown sugar
1/4 cup cane sugar
1 cup red wine
1/8 cup salt
1 tbsp. ground habanero pepper
1 large onion, chopped

Combine ingredients in a large bowl. Marinate ribs for about one hour. Smoke over medium hickory fire for about two hours. Baste every hour with marinade.

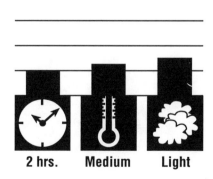

2 hrs.   Medium   Light

Kathleen's Ham

10-pound fully-cooked ham
20-30 whole cloves
1 small can pineapple slices
1/2 cup brown sugar

Drain juice from pineapple and mix with brown sugar. Take a sharp knife and draw a grid across ham. Place a clove in the center of each square. Place a couple of pineapple rings on top of the ham and pour the sugar mixture over all. Smoke for about two hours at 225 degrees. Ham isn't really barbeque, but it's cheap for a backyard party. And this recipe tastes pretty good.

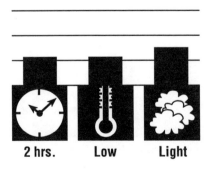

| 2 hrs. | Low | Light |

A-Dorr-Able Ribs

4 slabs St. Louis Cut Ribs
1 can Budweiser beer
2 tbsp. paprika
2 tbsp. salt
2 tbsp. mustard powder
1/4 cup brown sugar
2 tbsp. ground black pepper
2 tbsp. white pepper

Trim ribs, removing feather bones and brisket. Baste ribs with beer then sprinkle with spices. Top with brown sugar, then seal two slabs each in aluminum foil. Bake ribs in oven at 225 degrees for about two hours. Remove from oven and smoke over hickory fire for about two hours. Baste with beer every twenty minutes.

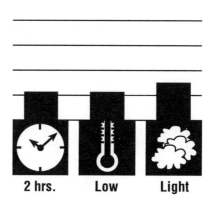

2 hrs.   Low   Light

Kim's Teriyaki Grilled Chicken

4 large chicken breasts
1/2 cup soy sauce
1/4 cup brown sugar
2 cloves garlic, pressed
2 tbsp. cracked black pepper
1/8 cup olive oil
1 tsp. ground ginger

Combine ingredients in a large bowl and allow to sit for about fifteen minutes. Pour over chicken and marinate for two hours. Place breasts on grill and cook for about an hour. Remove from heat, de-bone and return to grill for about another hour over a hickory fire.

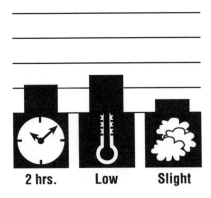

2 hrs.   Low   Slight

Baa Baa, Oink Oink Sausage

1 pd. boneless pork butt	2 cloves garlic, pressed
1 pd. boneless lamb shoulder	1/2 cup minced onion
	2 tbsp. cracked black pepper
1/4 cup lemon juice	1 tbsp. salt
1/4 cup olive oil	6 feet sausage casing
1/4 cup white wine	2 cans beer

Run pork and lamb through a meat grinder, then mix with the remaining ingredients. Stuff into casings. Place two cans of your favorite beer in a large disposable foil pan over a hot charcoal fire. Place sausage in beer. Cook until beer boils, about an hour and a half. Grill sausages over fire until brown, about 15 to 20 more minutes.

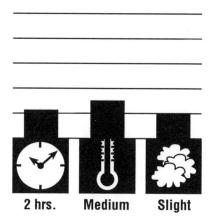

2 hrs.   Medium   Slight

Smoked Tenderloin of Beef

6-pound tenderloin
2 whole garlic cloves
1 tsp. ground rosemary
2 tbsp. cracked black pepper
1/2 cup olive oil
1/2 cup Italian Dressing

Rub tenderloin with olive oil, then rub with a mixture of garlic, rosemary and pepper. Place tenderloin on smoker and cook over hickory fire for about two hours or until the internal temperature reaches 150 degrees, for medium rare.

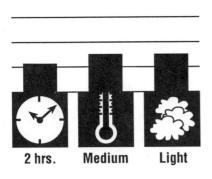

2 hrs.   Medium   Light

AB's Mutton

4 mutton chops, trimmed
1 tbsp. paprika
1 tbsp. mustard powder
1 tbsp. red pepper
1 tbsp. salt.
1 cup white vinegar

Soak chops in vinegar for about fifteen minutes. Mix spices in a small bowl. Sprinkle on both sides of chops. Smoke for about two hours over a hickory fire.

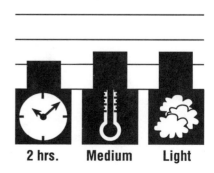

2 hrs.   Medium   Light

Smoked Lamb Shoulder

5 pounds lamb shoulder
1 tsp. paprika
1 tsp. rosemary
1/4 cup olive oil
1 tsp. cracked black pepper
1 tsp. salt
4 cloves garlic

Remove fat from lamb and place in a flat dish. Press garlic and combine with remaining ingredients in a medium sized bowl. Mix well and rub into lamb. Allow to marinate for about an hour. Smoke over hickory fire for about two hours.

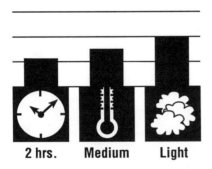

2 hrs.   Medium   Light

Barbequed Burittos

2 pounds pork butt
1 medium onion, sliced
1 whole clove garlic
1 tsp. salt
1/2 tsp. oregano, crushed

1/2 tsp. ground cumin
1 quart water
1 cup Guacamole
1 cup refried beans
1/2 cup salsa

Place pork in a disposable foil pan. Rub with salt, garlic, cumin and oregano. Cover with water, top with onions. Cook in a smoker with hickory wood for about two hours, or until pork shreds with a fork. Keep water level at least half way up on the pork. For each buritto, heat a tortilla on the grill until hot but not dry. Place about one half cup meat on tortilla and add two tablespoons Guacamole, three tablespoons beans and one tablespoon salsa for each buritto. Serve immediately.

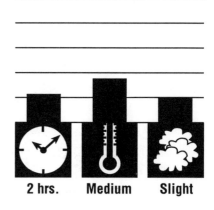

2 hrs.   Medium   Slight

Bob E.'s Boffo Burnt Ends

1 small brisket flat
1/4 cup dry rub
1/4 soy sauce
1/4 cup brown sugar
1/4 cup white vinegar

A small brisket should be about twelve inches long, and six to eight inches high. Trim so that no fat is remaining on the meat. Rub with vinegar and soy sauce, then slice into five or six equal portions. Roll each piece in dry rub and brown sugar. When slicing, cut on the same angle as the small tip of the brisket. Try to make each piece look as if it is the end. Smoke for about two hours over a medium fire or until tips begin to burn. Remove from smoker, cut into one inch cubes, top with your favorite barbecue sauce and serve.

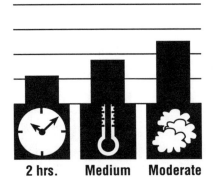

2 hrs.   Medium   Moderate

Smoked Salmon

1 large whole salmon
  (7-10 lbs.)
1/3 cup olive oil
1/4 cup lemon juice
1/3 cup white wine

1 large onion, sliced
1 tsp. salt
1 tbsp. black pepper
1 clove garlic
1/2 cup flour

Combine olive oil, lemon juice, wine, onion, salt, pepper and garlic.
Let stand for fifteen to twenty minutes, then pour over salmon. Allow
salmon to marinate for about ten minutes in the refrigerator. Drain fish
and lightly dust with flour. Brush with the remaining marinade. Place
on grill rack or foil away from fire and smoke for one and a half hours.
Brush with marinade while cooking. When skin begins to stick and pulls
away, smoke for another 30 minutes, for a total of about two hours.

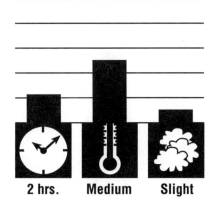

2 hrs.   Medium   Slight

Dr. Daniel's Fiery Pork Steak

4 pork steaks
2 tbsp. ground red pepper
2 tbsp. paprika
2 tbsp. crushed red pepper
2 tbsp. salt
2 tbsp. white pepper
1 tbsp. garlic powder
1 cup barbecue sauce

Rub seasoning into steaks. Grill for about seven minutes on each side. Move to cool side of grill cover and smoke for about an hour and thirty minutes, brushing with barbecue sauce every ten minutes.

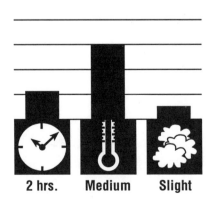

2 hrs.   Medium   Slight

Country Style Beef Ribs

2-4 pounds beef ribs
1/2 cup red wine vinegar
1 tbsp. oregano
1 tbsp. garlic powder
1 tbsp. white pepper
1 tbsp. salt
1/4 cup olive oil

Make a dry rub with oregano, pepper, garlic and salt. Rub ribs with oil and vinegar, then sprinkle with rub. Place on smoker with low, moist heat for two to three hours.

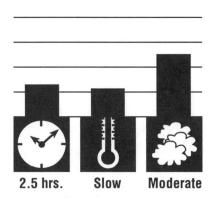

2.5 hrs.   Slow   Moderate

Robbie's Ribs

4 slabs baby back ribs
1/8 cup paprika
1/8 cup pepper
1/8 cup salt
1/8 cup sugar
2 cups Robbie's Rib Sauce[12]

Remove membrane from ribs. Make a dry rub with the paprika, pepper, salt and sugar. Rub generously on each slab. Tightly seal each slab in a piece of heavy-duty aluminum foil. Place the ribs on a cookie sheet and bake in oven for about two hours at 200 degrees. Remove from foil, place on grill or smoker with a hickory fire. Smoke ribs for about an hour and a half. Baste with Robbie's Rib Sauce every thirty minutes.

[12]Robbie's Rib Sauce — The recipe for this work of art can be found on page 142. You can also use your own favorite, but try Robbie's, for a great change of pace.

3 hrs.　　Slow　　Slight

Fritz's Flaming Pheasant

4 whole pheasants
1 cup lemon juice
1/4 cup sugar
1/2 cup white wine
1/2 cup Bacardi 151 Rum

Marinate birds in lemon juice, sugar, wine and half of rum for about three hours. Smoke over a low hickory fire for about three hours or until internal temperature reaches 165 degrees. Place on serving tray. Heat remaining 151 in microwave until very warm. Pour over birds and ignite. Present while flaming.

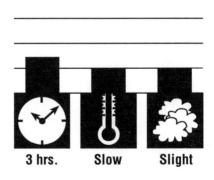

3 hrs.   Slow   Slight

Old Mill Gator

4 pounds fresh alligator
1 cup Old Mill BBQ Rub[13]
1/2 cup vinegar
1/2 cup olive oil

Soak gator meat in vinegar for about fifteen minutes. Coat thoroughly with Old Mill BBQ Rub. Seal in spices by rubbing with olive oil. Smoke over a hickory fire for about three hours. If gator begins to look dry, place in a pan with a few tablespoons of water. Smoke until water evaporates, about another thirty minutes.

[13]Old Mill Rib Rub — If unavailable in your area, you can create your own mixture. Combine 1/2 tsp. garlic powder, 1/2 tsp. onion powder, 1/4 cup worcestershire sauce, 1 tbsp. anchovy paste, 1 tbsp. ground black pepper, 1 tbsp. paprika, 1 tsp. ground red pepper, 1/8 cup brown sugar, and 1 tsp salt.

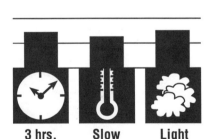

3 hrs.   Slow   Light

Spudly Beef Ribs

4 pounds country style beef ribs
4 pounds sliced russet potatoes
1/8 cup ground black pepper
1/8 cup salt
1/8 cup sugar
1/8 cup yellow mustard
1 cup butter or margarine

Rub ribs with pepper, salt and sugar. Smoke over a hickory fire for about two hours. Place ribs and potatoes on a grill rack and cover with a butter and mustard mixture. Smoke until potatoes are tender, about another hour.

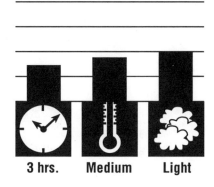

3 hrs.   Medium   Light

Absolute Smoked Turkey

10-15 lb. turkey
1/3 cup extra virgin olive oil
1/3 cup white wine
1/4 cup lemon juice
1 tsp. black pepper
1 tsp. salt
1 clove garlic (pressed)
1/2 cup onion (minced)
1 tsp. parsley

Combine all ingredients except turkey. Mix well and set aside to marinate for two to three hours in the refrigerator. Pour off marinade and smoke for about three hours. Use indirect grilling technique with foil or grill rack.

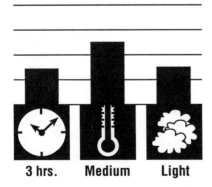

3 hrs.   Medium   Light

Dynamite Roast Beast

4-5 pound rump roast
1 cup red wine
2 tbsp. cracked black pepper
1 tsp. salt
1 tbsp. mustard powder
2 tsp. crushed red pepper

Combine wine, peppers, salt and mustard in a large bowl. Marinate roast for about thirty minutes. Smoke over hickory and mesquite fire until internal temperature reaches 160 degrees for medium. Baste with marinade while cooking.

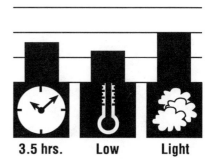

| 3.5 hrs. | Low | Light |

Tough to Beat Burnt Ends

5-pound brisket
1 cup Italian Dressing
1 tbsp. oregano
1/2 cup white wine
1/2 cup olive oil

Place brisket and all ingredients in a large ziplock bag. Shake well and marinate in refrigerator over night. Smoke over a hickory fire for about two hours. Split into three equal sections and smoke for two more hours. Burnt ends are traditionally the last part of the brisket, cubed or pulled, and served with your favorite sauce. The main feature is a heavy layer of charring, and the pink ring or smoke on the meat. The more sauce, the better.

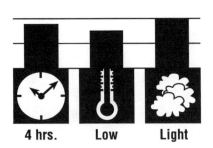

4 hrs.   Low   Light

Dijon Beef with Grilled Vegetables

2-4 pound top round
1/4 cup dijon mustard
1 cup red wine vinegar
1 whole clove garlic,
   pressed
1 tbsp. pepper
1/2 tbsp. salt

2 cups broccoli
2 cups carrots
2 cups new potatoes
2 cups green peppers
1 cup olive oil
1 cup Italian dressing

Mix dijon mustard, red wine vinegar, salt pepper and garlic. Spread on top round, and marinate for about one hour. Slice vegetables into bite sized pieces and coat generously with a mixture of olive oil and Italian dressing. Cook top round on smoker until internal temperature reaches 150 degrees. Add vegetables to smoker on a grill rack. Cook everything until meat reaches 160 degrees.

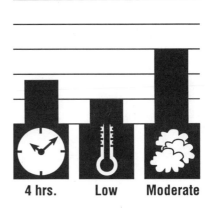

4 hrs.   Low   Moderate

Red Wine & Dijon Chicken

1 whole chicken, cut
1 cup red wine
1/2 cup dijon mustard
2 tbsp. cracked black pepper
1 tbsp. salt

Mix wine, mustard, salt and pepper. Spread over chicken parts and smoke over a low hickory fire for three to four hours. Brush with marinade every hour.

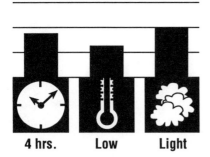

4 hrs.   Low   Light

Mad Dog's Ribs

6 slabs, 2-1/2 pounds and down
1 cup Rick's Rib Rub[14]
2 cups white vinegar
1 quart water
6 tbsp. olive oil

Trim and peel membrane from ribs. Rub generously with white vinegar, sprinkle lightly with Rib Rub, then pour one tablespoon of olive oil on each slab. Rub well. Combine remaining Rib Rub with remaining vinegar and water to form a baste. Smoke ribs over a hickory fire for four hours. Add hickory and baste every thirty minutes.

[14]Rick's Rib Rub — If unavailable in your area, you can create your own mixture. Combine 1 tsp. paprika, 1/2 tsp. ground red pepper, 1/2 tsp. ground black pepper, 1 tsp. salt, 2 tsp. sugar and 2 tbsp. brown sugar. Mix a large batch and use as needed with your favorite backyard recipes.

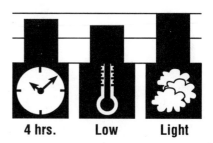

4 hrs.   Low   Light

Sharky's Ribs

4 slabs, baby back ribs
2 cups white vinegar
1/8 cup paprika
1/8 cup ground red pepper
1/8 cup ground
   black pepper

1/8 cup salt
1/8 cup brown sugar
1/8 cup cane sugar
2 tbsp. garlic powder
2 tbsp. onion powder
2 cups water

Remove membrane from back of ribs. Sprinkle with one cup of vinegar and rub well. Make a dry rub with all of the spices. Mix well. Use half of mixture to rub on to both sides of ribs. Place ribs over hickory fire for four to six hours at 225 degrees. Combine water, one cup vinegar and remaining spices and shake well in a bottle. Baste ribs with mixture every hour.

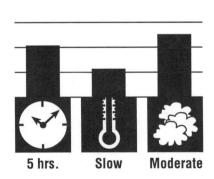

5 hrs.   Slow   Moderate

Bone's World Tour Honey Ribs

4 slabs, baby back ribs
1/4 cup paprika
1/4 cup red pepper
1/4 cup salt
1/8 cup black pepper
1/8 cup sugar
1 cup white vinegar
1 cup clover honey

Peel membrane from back of ribs. Rub generously with vinegar. Make a rub with the spices and generously rub into both sides of ribs. Smoke slowly over a hickory fire for about six hours. Sprinkle with remaining vinegar every hour. Cook ribs, stacking on top or each other. Rotate every hour. During last hour, drizzle honey on each slab.

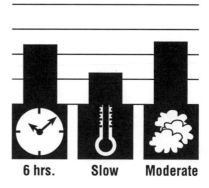

6 hrs.   Slow   Moderate

Lengthy
Leisure

3RD DEGREE
SPECIALTIES

R&B Tag-team Pork Tenderloin

2 pounds pork tenderloin
1/4 cup Italian Dressing
1/8 cup Backyard Lemon Butter Seasoning[15]
1 tsp. paprika
1 tsp. white pepper
1 tsp. ground black pepper
1 tsp. salt
1/4 cup white vinegar
1/4 cup olive oil

Rub tenderloin with olive oil and vinegar. Make a dry rub with paprika, peppers and salt, and rub into pork loin. Smoke for about one hour with hickory and peach wood. Combine Italian dressing and lemon butter. Spread over loin after first hour of smoking, then smoke for another hour or until internal temperature of 160 degrees.

[15]Backyard Lemon Butter Seasoning — If unavailable in your area, you can create your own mixture. Combine 1/4 cup lemon juice, 1/4 cup melted butter, 1 tsp. ground dill, and 1 tsp. garlic salt. Mix a large batch and use as needed with your favorite backyard recipes.

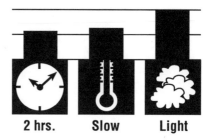

| 2 hrs. | Slow | Light |

Mandarin Orange & Lemon Chicken

4 large chicken breasts
1/2 cup mandarin oranges
1/2 cup lemon juice
1 clove garlic, pressed
1 tsp. salt
1 tsp. white pepper

Mix oranges, lemon juice, and garlic. Sprinkle salt and pepper on chicken, then spread with orange sauce. Allow to marinate for two hours. Smoke over apple and cherry wood fire for two to three hours or until temperature reaches 160 degrees. Make sure to prop up breasts with their bones, using indirect cooking method.

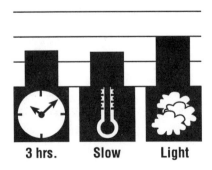

3 hrs.   Slow   Light

Ralph's Prime Rib

4-6 bone standing rib roast
1/2 cup worcestershire sauce
2 cloves garlic
1/4 cup olive oil
2 tbsp. black pepper
1/8 cup beef broth

Rub rib with olive oil. Rub with worcestershire sauce. Rub with beef broth. Crush garlic and pepper and rub into rib. Allow rib to sit in mixture for two hours, turning often. Drain and save mixture for basting on the grill. Place rib on indirect grill for about four hours, or until temperature reaches 160 degrees for medium rare. Baste every hour.

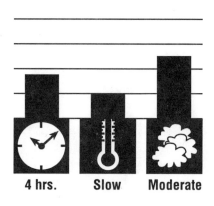

4 hrs.   Slow   Moderate

City Market Special Leg of Lamb

1 whole leg of lamb
4 whole cloves garlic
1 cup olive oil
1/8 cup cracked black pepper

Trim fat from leg. Peel garlic and cut cloves into small pieces. Cut one-inch deep holes in leg and stuff garlic into holes. Leg should be well covered with holes and garlic. Rub with olive oil and sprinkle with pepper. Smoke over apple and hickory fire for three to four hours or until internal temperature reaches 160 degrees in thickest part of leg. Serve with a mint sauce.

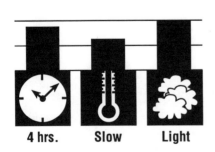

4 hrs.   Slow   Light

Wild Bill's Pork Tenderloin

2 pounds pork tenderloin
1 cup white vinegar
1 cup olive oil
1 cup white wine
2 tbsp. crushed red pepper
2 tbsp. salt
1/4 cup worcestershire sauce

Soak loin in vinegar for about thirty minutes. Add wine and olive oil and marinate for another thirty minutes. Drain and roll in salt and crushed red pepper. Smoke over a low hickory fire for about five hours. Baste with worcestershire sauce every hour.

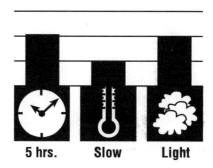

| 5 hrs. | Slow | Light |

Two Dollar A Pound "Prime Rib"

10-12 pound Top Sirloin Butt
5 ounces No Misteaks Marinade[16]
1/2 cup white vinegar
1 cup hot water
2 ounces No Misteaks Seasoning[17]

A whole top sirloin butt can be bought for about two dollars per pound at most "wholesale club" stores. Bring the sirloin to room temperature. Mix steak marinade, vinegar and water, and allow to sit for about five minutes. Place butt in a large mixing bowl, pour mixture over sirloin. Allow to marinate for about one hour. Smoke over hickory fire, until the internal temperature of the sirloin reaches 160 degrees. Sprinkle seasoning on fire while cooking and at table when serving.

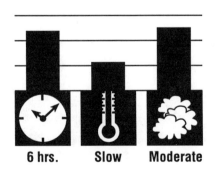

6 hrs.   Slow   Moderate

[16]No Misteaks Marinade — If unavailable in your area, you can create your own mixture. Combine 1 part worcestershire sauce, 1 part B-V Beef Broth, 1 part garlic powder, 1 part ground black pepper, and 1 part salt. Mix a large batch and use as needed with your favorite backyard recipes.

[17]No Misteaks Seasoning — If unavailable in your area, you can create your own mixture. Combine 1 part garlic powder, 1 part ground onion powder, 1 part ground black pepper, and 1 part salt. Mix a large batch and use as needed with your favorite backyard recipes.

Sharky's Turkey Breast

4 pound boneless turkey breast
1 cup white vinegar
2 tbsp. paprika
2 tbsp. salt
2 tbsp. red pepper
2 tbsp. garlic powder
2 tbsp. olive oil

Rub turkey with vinegar, then sprinkle with dry spices. Be sure to rub spices into all surfaces and under skin. Seal spices in by rubbing with olive oil. Smoke for four to six hours or until internal temperature reaches 170 degrees.

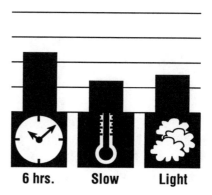

6 hrs.   Slow   Light

George's Smoked Turkey Breast

2 large turkey breasts
1/4 cup seasoning salt
3 tbsp. pepper
3 tbsp. paprika
2 tbsp. garlic powder
3 tbsp. chili powder
1 cup white vinegar
1 cup olive oil

Rub breasts inside and out with vinegar, let stand for fifteen minutes. Repeat process with olive oil and let stand for fifteen minutes. Make a dry rub with seasoning salt, pepper, paprika, garlic powder, and chili powder. Rub breasts inside and out, refrigerate overnight. Smoke over a fruitwood fire for five to six hours, or until internal temperature reaches 170 degrees.

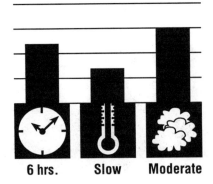

6 hrs.   Slow   Moderate

George's Smoked Pork Roast

5 pound pork shoulder or butt
1 cup sugar
1/4 cup seasoning salt
5 tbsp. pepper
3 tbsp. chili powder
2 tsp. allspice
3 tbsp. paprika
1 tsp. marjoram
1 1/2 tbsp. garlic powder
2 cups white vinegar

Cover pork with vinegar, let stand for thirty minutes. Make a dry rub with the remaining ingredients, rub into pork and refrigerate overnight. Smoke over a hickory fire for six to eight hours, or until internal temperature reaches 170 degrees.

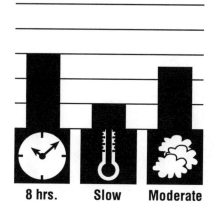

8 hrs.   Slow   Moderate

Andy's Jerked Deer

5 pound deer butt or shoulder
1 cup Jamaican Jerk Spice[18]
1 cup vinegar
1 cup worcestershire sauce

Marinate deer in vinegar and worcestershire for about one hour. Drain and rub generously with jerk spice. Smoke over a cherry wood fire for about eight hours.

[18]Jerk Spice — Combine 1 tbsp. ground allspice, 1 tsp. paprika, 1 tsp. crushed red pepper, 1/2 tsp. ground white pepper. Better yet, see if you can get a prepared blend from a gourmet store.

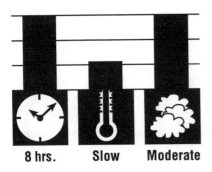

8 hrs.   **Slow**   **Moderate**

Lemon & Garlic Leg of Lamb

1 5-6 lb. leg of lamb
1/4 cup olive oil
1/4 cup lemon juice
1 clove garlic, pressed
1 tbsp. black pepper
1/2 tsp. salt

Remove excess fat from lamb, and place chops in large bowl. Combine ingredients in a small bowl and allow to sit at room temperature for about ten minutes. Pour mixture over chops and rub thoroughly. Cover with plastic wrap, and marinate for four to six hours. Grill over hot coals for about seven minutes on each side, then slow smoke over apple wood for about eight hours.

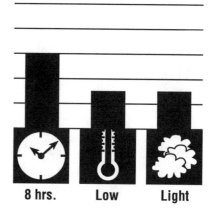

8 hrs.   Low   Light

Sharky's Honey Mustard Ham

1 raw ham
2 cups Sharky's Mustard Sauce[19]
1/2 cup honey

Completely cover ham with mustard sauce. Smoke over hickory fire for about 6 hours. Pour honey over ham and slow smoke for two to three more hours.

[19]Sharky's Mustard Sauce — This fabulous creation can be found on page 144, or you can use your own mustard recipe. Try Sharky's recipe just once, it takes a bite out of anything you've ever had.

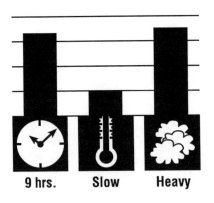

9 hrs.   **Slow**   **Heavy**

Rick's Rib Rub Brisket

12 pound brisket
1 cup worcestershire sauce
1/2 cup vinegar
1 cup Rick's Rib Rub[20]
1/4 cup No Misteaks Marinade[21]
1/4 cup No Misteaks Seasoning[22]

Trim fat, leaving a quarter of an inch on. Soak brisket in worcestershire sauce, vinegar and steak marinade, for about thirty minutes. Rub with Steak Seasoning and Rib Rub. Smoke for about 10 hours at 250 degrees.

[20]Rick's Rib Rub — If unavailable in your area, you can create your own mixture. Combine 1 tsp. paprika, 1/2 tsp. ground red pepper, 1/2 tsp. ground black pepper, 1 tsp. salt, 2 tsp. sugar and 2 tbsp. brown sugar. Mix a large batch and use as needed with your favorite backyard recipes.

[21]No Misteaks Marinade — If unavailable in your area, you can create your own mixture. Combine 1 part B-V Beef Broth, and 1 part Lea & Perrin Sauce. Mix a large batch and use as needed with your favorite backyard recipes.

[22]No Misteaks Marinade Seasoning — If unavailable in your area, you can create your own mixture. Combine 1/2 tsp. garlic powder, 1/2 tsp. ground onion powder, 1/2 tsp. ground black pepper, and 1/2 tsp. salt. Mix a large batch and use as needed with your favorite backyard recipes.

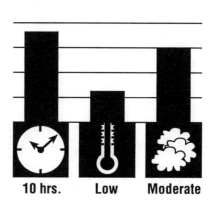

10 hrs.   Low   Moderate

Sharky's Brisket

12-pound brisket
2 cups worcestershire sauce
1 cup vinegar
1/8 cup paprika
1/8 cup salt
1/8 cup ground red pepper
1/8 cup beef broth
1/4 cup sugar
1/8 cup ground black pepper
1/8 cup brown sugar

Remove excess fat from meat. Combine all other ingredients in a large bowl, let stand for about thirty minutes. Soak brisket for about an hour in the mixture. Smoke brisket over a hickory fire for ten to twelve hours. Baste with marinade every two hours.

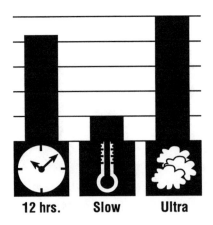

12 hrs.   Slow   Ultra

GJD I & II – Fool Proof Beef Brisket

10-pound brisket
1/4 cup lemon pepper
3 tbsp. MSG

Trim brisket so that about one eighth of an inch of fat remains. Remove large knot of fat from top of brisket. Cover brisket with lemon pepper and MSG. Slow smoke over hickory fire for ten to twelve hours.

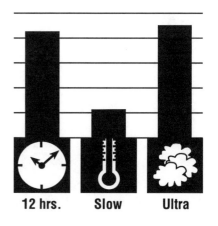

12 hrs.   Slow   Ultra

Honey & Garlic Smoked Brisket

8-pound brisket
1 cup clover honey
4 cloves garlic
4 tbsp. coarse black pepper

Remove most of fat from brisket. Cover with pressed garlic and pepper. Place on smoker fat side up. Cover with honey and smoke with hickory fire for 12 to 14 hours.

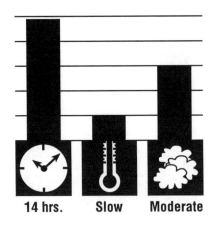

14 hrs.   Slow   Moderate

Pineapple Beach Brisket

10-pound brisket
1 cup brown sugar
1 cup crushed pineapple
1 tbsp. paprika
1 tbsp. chili pepper

Remove excess fat from brisket, but leave some on for flavor. Combine pineapple, brown sugar, paprika and pepper and spoon onto brisket. Smoke, pineapple side up for about 14 hours or until internal temperature reaches 160 degrees in thickest part of brisket.

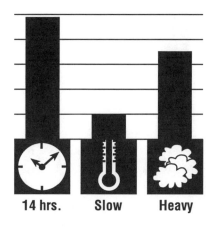

14 hrs.   Slow   Heavy

AB's Pseudo Brisket

4-pound chuck roast
1/2 cup No Misteaks Marinade[23]
1/4 cup worcestershire sauce
1/4 cup generic dry rub

Soak roast for about an hour in steak marinade and worcestershire sauce. Drain mixture and save for basting. Rub roast with dry rub and smoke over hickory fire for about sixteen hours. Baste every two hours with marinade mixture. Slice very thinly across grain like a brisket.

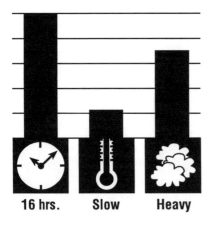

16 hrs.   Slow   Heavy

[23]No Misteaks Marinade — If unavailable in your area, you can create your own mixture. Combine 1 part B-V Beef Broth, and 1 part Lea & Perrin Sauce. Mix a large batch and use as needed with your favorite backyard recipes.

Marathon Brisket

14 lbs. brisket, untrimmed
1 cup olive oil
1/3 cup ground black pepper
1/3 cup brown sugar
1/2 cup paprika
1/4 cup cayenne pepper

Combine spices in a large bowl and set aside. Rub brisket with olive oil, then with spice mixture. Smoke over slow hickory fire for 10 hours. Remove from smoker and wrap in plastic film. Wrap again in aluminum foil. Return to smoker for another six hours. Remove and let stand for several minutes before thinly slicing.

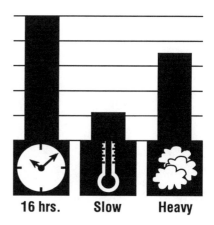

16 hrs.   Slow   Heavy

SAUCES, RUBS AND MARINADES

Big Bill's Favorite Steak Marinade

1 bottle BV Beef Broth
1/2 cup worcestershire sauce
1/4 cup white vinegar
1 tsp. garlic powder
1 tbsp. black pepper

Combine ingredients in a small bowl and allow to sit for fifteen minutes. Pour half of mixture over steaks, turn steaks and pour remainder of mixture. Allow steaks to marinate for fifteen minutes before grilling. This batch is enough for four Kansas City Strip Steaks, or two, inch and a half, center cut sirloin steaks.

Black & Blue Rub

1 tbsp. black mustard seed
1 tbsp. cracked black pepper
1 tbsp. cayenne pepper
1 tbsp. kosher salt
1/2 tbsp. yellow mustard powder
1/2 tbsp. ground ginger
1/2 tsp. ground black pepper
1/2 tsp. white pepper
1/2 cup brown sugar
1/4 cane sugar

Combine all ingredients, grind into a powder. For use as an interesting alternative to ordinary rubs.

Grapefruit & Honey Marinade

1/4 cup grapefruit juice
1 tbsp. grated grapefruit peel
1 tsp. ground red pepper
1/2 tsp. cayenne
1/4 cup honey
1/8 cup olive oil

Combine all ingredients in a bowl and stir until well blended. Great for use on poultry or pork.

Mad Dog's Rib Rub

1/4 cup paprika
1/4 cup red pepper
1/4 cup black pepper
1/4 cup white sugar
1/4 cup brown sugar
1 tbsp. garlic powder
1 tbsp. white pepper
1 tbsp. cayenne pepper

Combine ingredients in a covered bowl, mix well. Use about two tbsp. of rub for each side of rib slab. Rub slab generously with white vinegar before adding rub. It kicks in the rub.

Orange & Cranberry Marinade

1 cup water
1 cup fresh cranberries
1/8 cup honey
2 tsp. orange zest
1/8 cup fresh orange juice
1/2 cup white zinfandel
1/2 tsp. salt
1 tsp. ground black pepper

In a saucepan, combine cranberries, honey and water. Bring to a boil and simmer until cranberries are soft. Strain mixture through a sieve or fruit press, reserving juice for the marinade. Add remaining ingredients and simmer over low heat for about five minutes. Chill until needed. One batch is enough for two large chicken breasts.

Rick's Generic Dry Rub

1/4 cup paprika
1/4 cup black pepper
1/4 cup salt

Combine these ingredients in a small bowl, mix well. This rub can be used on any barbequed item. Just sprinkle lightly on the intended food, and rub. For a spicy taste, sprinkle more heavily. This batch will do about six to eight slabs of pork ribs. Use this rub as a base, add your favorite dry spices to make your smoker the best on the block.

Sweet & Sour BBQ Marinade

1 cinnamon stick
1 tsp. ginger root
1/2 tsp. cloves
1/2 tsp. mustard seed
1/2 tsp. cayenne pepper
1 tsp. black peppercorns
1/8 cup honey
1/8 cup sherry
1/8 cup tomato paste
1 clove garlic, pressed
1/8 cup soy sauce

Grind ginger, cloves, mustard, cayenne, and peppercorns, with a mortal and pestle, until thoroughly blended. Combine with remaining ingredients in a medium bowl. Stir until well blended. Use on ribs, pork or chicken.

Boiling BBQ Sauce

1 cup distilled water
1/2 cup green chili sauce
1/2 cup red chili sauce
1/2 cup A-1 Sauce
1/2 cup white vinegar
1/2 cup brown sugar
1 tbsp. chili powder
1 tbsp. celery seed
1 tbsp. salt
1 tbsp. ground black pepper
1 tbsp. habanero pepper sauce
1 tbsp. onion powder

Combine all ingredients in a large sauce pan. Bring to a boil, remove from heat. Use this sauce to bring your BBQ to life. It will "boil" long after its been removed from the stove.

George's BBQ Sauce

1 28 ounce bottle catsup
14 ounces water
1 tbsp. prepared mustard
2 tbsp. worcestershire sauce
1 tsp. Red Devil Pepper Sauce
1 tbsp. black pepper
1 tbsp. salt
2 tbsp. brown sugar
2 tbsp. lemon juice
1 medium onion, diced

Pour catsup into a saucepan. Fill empty bottle half way with water and shake well. Pour into saucepan. Add mustard stir and simmer. Add remaining ingredients, one at a time, stirring after each. Simmer for about thirty minutes.

Kinda Karolina Sauce

1 cup mustard
1 cup vinegar
1/4 cup red pepper
1/4 cup salt
1 cup water

Bring to a boil. Pour over anything that isn't moving.

Linda's KC Sauce

1 cup tomato paste
1 cup water
1/4 cup worcestershire sauce
1/4 cup white vinegar
1/2 cup molasses
1/2 cup brown sugar
1/4 cup onion flakes
1/8 cup paprika
2 tbsp. celery seed
1/8 cup salt
1/8 cup tabasco sauce
2 tbsp. cracked black pepper

Combine ingredients in order in a large saucepan. Stir well and simmer for about one hour.

Mad Dog B-B-Q Sauce

2 cups tomato paste
1 cup tomato sauce
1/4 cup white vinegar
1/2 cup molasses
1/4 cup Worcestershire Sauce
1 large onion
1/8 cup olive oil
1/8 cup brown sugar
4 cloves garlic
1 tbsp. dry mustard
1 tbsp. oregano
1 tsp. thyme

Chop onion fine, and simmer in olive oil until transparent. Mince garlic and add to onion, simmer for about another minute. Fold in remaining ingredients and bring to a boil. Simmer for about fifteen minutes. Store in refrigerator. Use on any barbecue specialty.

Old Fashion Beer-B-Q Sauce

1 cup tomato catsup
1 cup tomato paste
12 ounces beer
1/4 cup honey
1/8 cup soy sauce
1/8 cup lemon juice
2 cloves garlic
2 tbsp. paprika
1 tbsp. chili powder
1 tsp. salt

Smash garlic in a press or on waxed paper, until well pulverized. Combine garlic, paprika, chili powder and salt in a small bowl. Mix in lemon juice and soy sauce, stir until consistent. Add remaining ingredients and store in a covered bowl for at least twenty four hours before use. Refrigeration is recommended.

Robbie's Rib Sauce

1 cup crushed pineapple
1 cup red wine vinegar
1 cup brown sugar
1/4 cup Madeira
1 green bell pepper, diced
1 tbsp. corn starch

Combine vinegar, sugar, pineapple, Madeira, and peppers in a sauce pan. Bring to a boil. Remove from heat, add corn starch to thicken. Stir well.

Scotty's Beam Me Up Sauce

1/2 cup maple syrup
1/2 cup bourbon whiskey
1/8 cup Rick's Rib Rub[24]
1/4 cup brown sugar
2 tbsp. ground black pepper
2 tbsp. salt
1 tsp. tabasco sauce
1 cup tomato juice
1/2 cup tomato paste
1/4 cup chopped onion
1/4 cup chopped green pepper
1/4 cup chopped celery

Chop onion, green pepper and celery into very fine bits. Combine all ingredients in a sauce pan and simmer for about thirty minutes. Keep heat low as to not burn sugars. Cool and refrigerate. Use on any barbecue item.

[24]Rick's Rib Rub — If unavailable in your area, you can create your own mixture. Combine 1 tsp. paprika, 1/2 tsp. ground red pepper, 1/2 tsp. ground black pepper, 1 tsp. salt, 2 tsp. sugar and 2 tbsp. brown sugar. Mix a large batch and use as needed with your favorite backyard recipes.

Sharky's Mustard Sauce

1 cup prepared yellow mustard
1 cup brown sugar
1/2 cup white vinegar
1 tbsp. paprika
1 tbsp. black pepper
1 tbsp. salt
1 tsp. garlic powder

Combine paprika, black pepper, salt and garlic and grind with a mortar and pestle, until fine. Combine all ingredients in a mixing bowl, stir until creamy. Chill for about fifteen minutes before use.

Wild Bill's Kansas City Sauce

1 cup KC Masterpiece Original Barbeque Sauce
1/2 cup Gates Original Classic Barbeque
1/4 cup white vinegar
1/8 cup Worcestershire Sauce
2 tbsp. Backyard BBQ & Grill Seasoning[25]

Combine all ingredients in a sauce pan and simmer over medium heat for about fifteen minutes. A tribute to KC's finest exports with a little spice for a kicker.

---

[25]BBQ & Grill Seasoning — If unavailable in your area, you can create your own mixture. Combine 1 part paprika, 1 part ground black pepper, and 1 part salt. Mix a large batch and use as needed with your favorite backyard recipes.

SIDE DISHES

Devilish Backyard Barbeque Eggs

24 hard boiled eggs
1 cup prepared yellow mustard
1 tsp. mustard powder
1 tsp. salt
1 tsp. paprika
1 tsp. garlic powder
1/4 cup mayonnaise
2 tbsp. dried onion flakes

Peel and cut eggs in half. Separate yolks and place them in a large mixing bowl. Place whites on a large cookie sheet to be filled later. Combine remaining ingredients with egg yolks and stir well. Spoon filling into egg whites and chill before serving. Garnish with paprika.

Kathleen's Potato Salad

10 pounds russet potatoes
12 eggs
2 cups mayonnaise
1 cup prepared yellow mustard
1 cup diced dill pickles
1 cup sliced celery
2 tbsp. coarse black pepper
2 tbsp. salt
1/2 cup diced onions

Hard boil eggs, and boil potatoes until they split. Allow eggs and potatoes to cool, then dice into small chunks. Combine all ingredients in a large mixing bowl. More mayonnaise and mustard may be added for a moist salad. Chill before serving.

Lil's Cole Slaw

4 cups shredded cabbage
1/2 cup diced celery
1/2 cup shredded carrots
1/2 cup mayonnaise
1 tsp. salt
1 tbsp. ground black pepper
1/2 cup milk
1/4 cup shredded onion
1 tbsp. paprika

Combine ingredients in a large mixing bowl. Stir well, chill and serve. Top with paprika and more pepper as a garnish.

Julie's Potato Casserole

1 bag, shredded hash brown potatoes
1 cup cream of chicken soup
1/2 cup sour cream
1/4 cup milk
2 cups shredded cheddar cheese

Mix potatoes with soup, sour cream, milk and one cup of cheese. Stir well, then spread mixture in a ten inch glass casserole dish. Top with remaining cheese, salt and pepper. Bake in over until cheese bubbles, or at 350 degrees for thirty minutes.

Smoked Pumpernickel Salad

4 small pumpernickel loaves
1/2 pound cooked turkey breast
1/2 pound cooked ham
1 small onion
2 stalks celery
1/2 cup Monterey Jack cheese
1/2 cup cheddar cheese
1/2 tsp. paprika
1/2 tsp. pepper
1/2 tsp. salt
1/2 tsp. ground red pepper
4 tbsp. mayonnaise

Hollow out as bowls four pumpernickel loaves. A five- to six-inch loaf is fine. In a mixing bowl, combine the remaining ingredients with half of each cheese. Mix well and stuff loaves with mixture. Top with remainder of cheese. Smoke using indirect method for about one hour or until cheese is melted.

Jane E.'s Twice Bakes

4 large baking potatoes
1 cup cheddar cheese
1 cup mozzarella cheese
1 cup sour cream
1 tbsp. garlic powder
1/2 cup butter or margarine
1 tbsp. ground black pepper
1 tsp. salt
1 tbsp. onion flakes

Bake potatoes for one hour at 400 degrees. Remove from oven and cut each in half. Spoon out skin, leaving one eighth inch of potato on skin. Combine hot inside pulp with half of cheeses and remaining ingredients. Mix well and scoop mixture into the potato shells. Mix remaining cheese in a plastic bag, shake well. Top stuffed potatoes with cheese and bake for thirty to forty five minutes at 300 degrees, or until cheese melts.

Heartland Bar-B-Cue Beans

2 quarts pork and beans
1/4 cup Backyard BBQ & Grill Seasoning[26]
1 cup brisket burnt ends
1/2 cup prepared yellow mustard
1 cup Heartland Bar-B-Cue Sauce
1 onion

In a large pan combine beans, seasoning, mustard and sauce. Finely chop onion and brisket burnt ends and stir into beans. Place pan in smoker or grill, and smoke uncovered for two to four hours, using hickory wood.

[26]BBQ & Grill Seasoning — If unavailable in your area, you can create your own mixture. Combine 1 part paprika, 1 part ground black pepper, and 1 part salt. Mix a large batch and use as needed with your favorite backyard recipes.

Not "So Burnt" Endings

DESSERTS

Barbecued Bananas

4 bananas, peeled
1/4 cup brown sugar
1/4 cup rum
2 tbsp. lemon juice
4 tbsp. butter or margarine
4 pieces aluminum foil

Soften butter and coat foil. Mix brown sugar, rum and lemon juice in a small dish. Coat each banana with rum mixture and wrap tightly in foil. Place on grill for about fifteen to twenty minutes.

Becerro's Kicker

1 large scoop coffee ice cream
1 1/2 ounce Kahlua
1/8 cup half & half
1 1/2 ounce vodka
2 tbsp. whipped cream
1 tsp. shaved chocolate

Combine ice cream, Kahlua, vodka and half & half in a blender. Mix until the consistency of a milk shake. Add more half & half if necessary. Pour into frozen juice or rocks glasses. Top with whipped cream and chocolate shavings.

Chilled Fruits in Wine Sauce

1 cup cantaloupe balls
1 cup watermelon balls
1 cup strawberries
1 cup green grapes
1 cup banana slices
1 cup white wine
1/4 cup sugar
1/8 cup lime juice
6 tsp. powdered sugar

Mix wine, sugar and lime juice in a small dish. Place fruit in stem up glasses, and freeze for about twenty minutes. Pour wine sauce over fruit and top with one teaspoon of powdered sugar.

Dancing Angel Food Lemon Cake

1 angel food cake, your favorite
1 cup lemon juice
1/8 cup amaretto
1/8 cup vodka
1/2 cup powdered sugar

Make a glaze with lemon juice, sugar, vodka and amaretto. Drizzle over angel food cake and chill. Serve and you'll be dancing for dessert.

Flaming Cherry Cheese Cake

1 cheese cake, your favorite
1 can, cherry pie filling
1/4 cup amaretto
1 tbsp. cinnamon
1/8 cup Kirsh
1/4 cup Bacardi 151 Rum

Prepare your favorite cheese cake, or buy one at the store. Combine cherries, amaretto, cinnamon and ginger in a saucepan, simmer. When warm, place mixture in a large flat glass dish. Warm 151 in a saucepan or in microwave. Pour 151 over cherries, and ignite. Present and serve while flaming.

Grilled Ice Cream

1/2 cup chocolate syrup
1/8 cup Kahlua
1/8 cup Frangelico
1/4 cup chocolate liqueur
1 quart vanilla ice cream
1/4 cup powdered sugar

Mix chocolate syrup, sugar and liqueurs in a small saucepan. Scoop ice cream into stoneware dishes and top with chocolate mixture, coat ice cream evenly. Freeze for about two hours. Place dishes on a cookie sheet and put in covered grill until ice cream begins to melt. Serve immediately. With a hot fire, about two to three minutes is enough time on the grill.

Strawberries a la Ralph

1 quart fresh strawberries
1/8 cup amaretto
1/8 cup Grand Marnier
1/8 cup vodka
1/4 cup powdered sugar
1/8 cup Bacardi 151 Rum

Chill strawberries for about thirty minutes in the freezer. Mix amaretto, vodka and powdered sugar in a small dish. Add Grand Marnier and chill. Warm 151 in microwave. Place strawberries in chilled dishes, top with amaretto mixture. Top again with 151 and ignite. Serve flaming.

INDEX

INDEX

INDEX

INDEX

INDEX

INDEX